"It's never been more important than right now to learn some essential recipes on how to free up cashflow and increase your savings. Thank goodness for *Cashflow Cookbook*, which provides more than the traditional money-saving tips we've all heard a million times before, but instead creative techniques and detailed action-steps on how to improve your financial present and future one dollar at a time."

Jessica Moorhouse, AFCC®, Money Expert, Financial Educator, Owner & CEO of MoorMoney Media Inc

"As a wealth advisor, I help my clients optimize every aspect of their finances. *Cashflow Cookbook* and Gordon's talks add another layer of value. His financial recipes unlock more cashflow for investing. Practical, useable ideas that anyone can adopt to transform their finances. Buy this book!"

Aaron M. Vaughn, JD, CFP®, BFA™, APMA®, Life Planning Pathfinder, Defiant Services LLC

"Compound interest truly is an amazing thing. If you don't believe Gordon, maybe Einstein or Buffet can convince you. The truth is every dollar you save and invest today will go much further in retirement. Gordon's book is full of ideas that will allow anyone who puts in the effort to retire with substantially more money."

Nicholas Daniel, Co-founder, Columbus Wealth Management

"An awesome read! Finally, there's a financial planning book that doesn't leave the reader feeling overwhelmed, discouraged, and restricted. *Cashflow Cookbook* releases us from financial worry and helps us live joyfully and abundantly. I was privileged to interview Gordon on my podcast, where he shared a wealth of powerful information to help my listeners improve their financial wellbeing. I highly recommend *Cashflow Cookbook* to anyone who wants to become financially free."

Linda Bjork, bestselling author and host of Linda's Corner Podcast

"A new book on personal finance that a financial coach like myself can employ to assist my clients in getting out of debt and improving their life. Gordon's practical concepts in the book are applicable to all individuals and may be implemented immediately. Purchase Gordon's book today, and you'll be well on your way to a better financial future."

Ryan DeMent, Managing Partner, TruVest and host of Chasing Financial Freedom *Podcast*

Cashflow Cookbook

US Edition

Cashflow Cookbook

US Edition

$2 Million of Financial Freedom
in 60 Easy Recipes

Gordon Stein
Brookside Wealth LLC

Published by Brookside Wealth LLC
Cleveland, OH
CashflowCookbook.com

Printed Edition: ISBN: 979-8-9863066-0-5
First printing June 2022

Developmental editing by Elizabeth Williams
Copy edited by Linda Popky
Cover designed by Shena Honey Lagapa Pulido

Page layout by Sheila Mahoney

Important Note to Readers
The contents of this book are for general information only. This book presents ideas for handling many situations that may require a professional advisor, counsellor, technician, or tradesperson (an "expert"). This book is not a substitute for the involvement of an expert in your specific situation. Before applying general information to your own situation, always consult an expert with the qualifications needed in your circumstances. Failure to do so may result in harm. The author is writing based on his own experience. Applying the author's ideas and experience to your specific situation may produce results that differ from the author's results. Results may vary from person to person. This book is not intended to solicit the sale of any investment or financial or insurance product. Any similarity or resemblance of characters to persons living or deceased in any of the anecdotes or scenarios presented is purely coincidental.

Dedicated to the memory of my mother, Thelma Barer-Stein, who gave me a lifelong love of learning, reading, and writing.

Table of Contents

Foreword

I met Gordon back in the nineties when we both worked at a high-tech firm. He was a senior vice president and I was just starting my career after earning an undergraduate degree in Psychology—and I was trying to figure out what to do with it!

Although Gordon was an outstanding sales and marketing executive, those who have had the pleasure of working with him know that, like a favorite teacher in high school, he truly excels as a mentor, coach, and storyteller. Luckily for me and my colleagues (whether Gordon knows it or not), I think we earned the equivalent of a master's degree in human psychology from him. He not only has a knack for unlocking challenging issues, but also has the ability to help you resolve them with solutions that you are inspired to implement—while having fun along the way.

As our careers rolled on, I transitioned into financial services where I earned my Certified Financial Planner (CFP) and Chartered

Investment Manager (CIM) professional designations. My path led me to leadership roles at wealth management firms, where I've trained, managed, and supervised teams of financial advisors and discretionary investment portfolio managers. Over the course of my career working with many of these outstanding professionals, it's clear to me that the most successful advisors are effective at helping their clients align their financial behavior with their most important goals and most deeply held values. This is easier said than done. Helping clients adjust their financial behavior so that they can achieve the life they envision is one of the hardest and least talked about things that great financial advisors do really well for their clients.

Adding to the challenge for financial advisors, individuals, and families is the fact that there's not a lot of material out there that teaches non-budget based, easy-to-implement ways to modify financial spending habits—habits that, with a just a few mindful adjustments like the ones Gordon teaches in this book, can lead to life-changing outcomes.

So why is changing your financial spending behavior so difficult? Because people like spending, they don't like saving, and they hate budgeting! There are actually deeply rooted physiological and neurochemical reasons for this, driven by our body's production of dopamine, serotonin, oxytocin, and endorphins.

These are our brain's pleasure-generating "reward chemicals" and they deliver the feelings of well-being we describe as happiness, as well as other human sensations and emotions.

Our brains produce a rush of dopamine when we shop, analogous to the experience of "gathering" that is a survival-supporting behavior our physiology evolved to reward us. Our bodies produce serotonin when we both give and receive care to and from others, which is why we feel good entertaining or going out for dinner to fine restaurants. We get the added benefit of a pleasurable dopamine response from eating and drinking.

Although we could watch sports events on TV, we spend money on live event tickets to get the rush of oxytocin from being present with massive groups of like-minded sports fans cheering for the same team in the same large stadiums or arenas. This is a tribal survival-in-numbers behavior that our brains evolved to produce oxytocin to reward. The point here is that we are hard-wired by our neurophysiology to spend for any number of reasons that seem to all be encouraged by our brain chemical-driven survival instincts.

So how do we stop? The answer is don't even try. Just as Noom uses psychology to help us lose weight by eating more mindfully, Gordon's *Cashflow Cookbook* helps us save more by showing us how to spend more mindfully!

Regardless of income level, it's human nature to spend more than what we make, leaving us controlled by money instead of empowered by it to fund the experiences in life that really matter to us most. If that sounds familiar, and you want to gain back financial control of your life, the good news is that this book shows you how to save without even noticing it. Some may even call this saving without behaving.

It's no surprise to me that Gordon is now applying his talent to help a much broader base of people, companies, and professional advisors with this book, supported by his speaking and consulting engagements. In doing so, he is helping those who are looking for practical solutions that directly address one of the most challenging areas of personal and family finance—cash flow management. This is not only one of the most overlooked areas of professional financial advice, but also one of the most important things financial planners can address to better serve their clients and add differentiating value to their practice.

For young people, this book is a way to start on the right financial track, save and invest more, and use the power of compounding to build wealth and freedom. For those in their mid-career, here's the solution to tame the heavy spending years and build a solid financial footing. For those contemplating retirement, this book is a way to maximize lifestyle while taming your burn rate. For financial planners and advisors, this is THE book to give your clients to help them increase their savings rate, build their wealth faster, and help them make their money last longer.

Gordon wrote *Cashflow Cookbook,* to provide a breakthrough way to free up more cashflow for debt repayment or investing, without giving up things or having to budget. He applies his personal teaching style and wit to an easy-to-read volume of financial behavior adjustments that he calls "recipes" anyone can use to dramatically improve their finances. In doing so, Gordon provides easy steps to take back financial control in your life—or for advisors, to help others gain financial control so they can live happier, healthier, and less stressful lives.

Ron Fox, CFP, CIM
CEO, Glidepath Portfolio Services Inc.

Preface

I'M WATCHING THE birds out my studio window in Cleveland, OH, a cup of coffee warming my hands and two cats near my feet. I glance at my weather app, which I use to plan my time when I don't have a speaking engagement or a writing deadline. If it's warm and sunny, that could mean a bike on the Rocky River Trail or a kayak on the nearby Cuyahoga River. Snow could mean a ski trip East to Ellicottville, NY. Or a longer one to Colorado. A rainy afternoon might suggest pulling one of my guitars off the wall and inviting my lead vocalist/wife in for a jam. Happy hour often starts at 5 or so. There is no HR department.

A personal finance discovery was a key enabler of my early retirement. I found an easy way for the average person to add $1 million or more to their wealth. It involves no budgeting. No tug of war between enjoy now and save for later. No high-tech knowledge or side hustles. Nothing else to buy. In total, it takes about ten hours of work that pretty much anyone can do. And yes, it really works.

In an ironic twist, the very discovery that brought me early retirement now keeps me busy helping others ease their financial stress and add millions to their wealth. I am back working again, but now on my own terms, doing things that are meaningful and fun. It's rewarding to help people with one of their biggest issues, their money. I am shocked at the state of our financial "wellness."

We live in the richest and most developed country in the world, yet we struggle with money. How bad is it? Let's look:

- **Stress:** Money is the top stressor for Americans.[1] In fact, 77% of Americans are anxious about their finances.[2]
- **Household:** Nearly two-thirds (64%) of Americans with children are living paycheck to paycheck.[3]
- **Workplace:** More than 70% of us report carrying our financial stress into the workplace.[4]
- **Emergencies:** Over one-third (35%) would have difficulty handling a $400 emergency expense.[5]
- **Car Ownership:** More Americans are accepting loans with payoff terms of 84 months. Only 21% of buyers look at the total interest paid when evaluating financing alternatives.[6]
- **College Debt:** Thirty-six percent of Americans are unaware of 529 plans (an efficient way to save for a college education) and only 20% of parents either use one or plan to.[7]
- **Divorce:** Money causes the most stress in relationships.[8]
- **Retirement:** Forty-five percent have no money set aside for retirement, while 19% said that they will retire with less

[1] Michelle Black, "Americans' Stress Levels – and Financial Anxiety – on the Rise," Valuepenguin.com, April 2022, https://bit.ly/3OOSeTF
[2] "Mind Over Money." capitalone.com, January 2020, https://bit.ly/3xuuUrV
[3] "Reality Check – The Paycheck-to-Paycheck report," pymnts.com, June 2021, https://bit.ly/3Jk5bo5
[4] Cody Puckett, "The Impact of Financial Stress in America,", hellospring.io, February 2020, https://bit.ly/3Jn2PFc
[5] "Report on the Economic Well-Being of U.S. Households in 2020 – May 2021, federalreserve.gov, https://bit.ly/3rbMFIy
[6] "Study: how are Americans buying cars?" lexingtonlaw.com, https://bit.ly/3NZDG71
[7] "10th Annual 529 Awareness Study," Edward Jones.com, May 17, 2021, https://bit.ly/3ujlFbP
[8] "Money Causes the Most Stress in Relationships," media.ally.com, June 2018, https://bit.ly/37sHHzW

than $10,000. In other words, these 64% of Americans will retire broke.[9]

In short, poor financial literacy impacts every aspect of our lives. I'm amazed at corporate wellness programs with comprehensive offerings aimed at *reducing workplace stress* that don't include a financial wellness component – the number one *cause of stress* in the first place.

But let's get back to my discovery and how it can be used to give you a lifetime of financial wellness without the need to give up things you love, endure a monthly budgeting process, or haggle over every expense.

It began with a car wash

Many years back, I was driving to a party with a friend. He spotted a car wash receipt on the floor mat and asked why I would spend money on car washes. It was a good question. But who has time to worry about the cost of car washes?

He went on to explain how the points he earned through a gas retailer loyalty program earned him free car washes. I nodded, but seriously, was I really going to sign up for the program, remember to swipe my loyalty card, go online somewhere to track points, and then fill in some form, all to collect a free wash? Then there was the issue of carrying one of those monster wallets stuffed with loyalty cards for every fish market, haircutting place, and oil change shop. Who needs it?

Driving to work one day, I heard an ad for a discount home alarm company. The catchy jingle caught my attention, and their price was about $25 cheaper each month than what I was paying. I remembered my friend's car wash idea, worth about the same $25

---

[9] "64% of Americans Aren't Prepared for Retirement - and 48% Don't Care," gobankingrates.com, September 2019, https://bit.ly/3vo5s4H

per month. I signed up for the gas loyalty program that day, and then called the alarm company. Between the two, my checking account was fatter by $50 a month.

OK, sure, it was only 50 bucks. But it was also incredibly easy. I got a gas loyalty card for my wife, and we saved another $25 a month. With minimal effort, we now had $75 each month of real savings.

I then did a bit of math to see how $75 a month might grow if I invested it at say 7%, for 20 years. Remarkably, it would reach $39,225. Wow. And after 40 years, that amount would stretch to an incredible $196,575. The median retirement savings for baby boomer Americans is only $202,000.[10] *So, a couple of simple changes offer a way to nearly double your wealth vs the average American.* And we're just getting started.

My engineer/MBA brain sprang to attention. How far could this go? Could these ideas add millions to the wealth of an average person? Turns out the answer is yes.

What else is there?

Over the next two years, I searched for these cashflow ideas like a pig hunting a truffle. I engaged in online research and personal experimentation, read emails from my blog readers, and did lots of canvassing. I made a list of ideas that could save at least $25 a month. Some saved as much as $900 per month. I discarded any that were too much work, too hard to implement, or didn't save enough.[11] I added up the value of all the savings ideas. It tallied $13,000. Yes, monthly.

---

[10] "Workers Are Saving for Retirement Despite Challenges Amid the Pandemic," Transamericacenter.org, August 2021, https://bit.ly/3Jp33vx
[11] If I wouldn't do it myself, it stayed off the list. So, no mixing home cleaning products, no tin foil on the windows to reduce air conditioning bills, and no coupon clipping.

The list became a spreadsheet as I calculated the future value of the savings invested over time. The numbers were huge. I took the spreadsheet to my accountant for an audit and waited to hear about the errors. Instead, he agreed with the math and said that it would make a great book.

As I started writing, this topic didn't fit as a novel or a parable. But it did click as a financial cookbook. First, this became a newspaper column. That led to a blog, a speaking career, and guesting on a lot of podcasts. Financial advisors now use this to help their clients free up more cash for investing. Students now have new tools to start on a path of financial wellness. Companies use the book and my talks to help employees with financial wellness—an often-overlooked part of an overall wellness program.

The book was published originally in my native Canada. Now that I'm living in the US, it's time for a US edition. As I did the research, it was clear that the opportunities to free up cashflow are even greater here. I'm excited to bring the concepts to my new country and a new audience.

The most important audience? You. These ideas can help you add a million dollars or more to your wealth and free you to focus your life on something meaningful. Grab a plate and a big helping of financial wellness.

Bon Appetit.

Introduction

I HAVE ENJOYED DOZENS of personal finance books. Some are on dividend investing. Others focus on the benefits of diversification or buying the companies from which you purchase products. Still others make the case for annuities, crypto, or rare art. Many begin with the idea of saving 10% of your income and investing it in something that will rise over time. All of these are great ideas.

But it feels like we are missing the book before those books. To invest, or even pay down debt, we are going to need some money. And for most of us, there's a shortage of the stuff. Sure, lots comes in, but where did it go? It's a familiar story for those earning $50,000 a year, and even to those earning $500,000 a year. The marketing machinery gains power each year: better slogans, targeted social media, functional MRI studies to learn how we buy, and easy payment plans to commit us to spend up to the limit of our income. Or well beyond. *We consumers gain things and lose wealth.*

And so, the gravy boat of financial security passes us by on the way around the table. We save a fraction of what we should. We gather less of what rises in value and too much of that which falls. We work longer than we need to. Chained to a paycheck to cover a bewildering assortment of bills, we may even miss our greater life purpose.

The usual solutions aren't that palatable. Keeping a budget to avoid overspending? Must we? Giving up things we love? Uh, no thanks. Embracing frugality and living in a micro house? No room for my kayak. The most effective approach is also the hardest to implement: picking wealthier parents.

So, all of that brings us here to the *Cashflow Cookbook*. The idea is simple. You'll learn how to free up more money for debt reduction or investing. A lot more. And you can do it with minimal effort, minimal sacrifice, and no budgeting.

In *Part I – The Banquet*, we'll meet a 40-year-old couple, Eric and Keisha. They will stumble into a series of financial discoveries that will accelerate their savings and completely change their financial trajectory. They'll unlock wealth that will let them consider life options: retire early, take a year sabbatical, increase their charitable donations, easily fund college for their twins, or just give them a plusher retirement. What will change in their lifestyle to make this possible? Pretty much nothing. Yes, really.

Some of you will follow along and copy their moves. Please do! Others may find that the changes that Eric and Keisha make aren't possible in their lives. Maybe you have a different situation or you're at a different life stage. No problem. Part I is just there to whet your appetite. That's why the book goes on to *Part II – The Recipes*. In this section, we'll look at 60 more financial "recipes" – ways to save on virtually every spending area. These recipes total a remarkable $13,000 monthly. Once those savings are in place, you'll want to "savor the savings" by making them work for you: paying down debt or increasing your investments.

Will you be able to save the full $13,000? Unlikely. For most, there should be at least $500 worth of monthly savings that you hadn't considered. Investing that at 7% for 30 years would add more than $613,000 to your wealth. Some may be able to free up

$2,000 which would net you close to $2.5 million over that same period. Let me know how you do.

I'm sure you're hungry to get started. Get ready to be served a tasty read and a delicious book investment—sandwiched between these covers.

Gordon Stein – Cleveland, Ohio, May 2022

Part 1 – The Banquet

Come to the dinner gong
The table is laden high
Fat bellies and hungry little ones
Tuck your napkins in
Take your share
Some get the gravy
And some get the gristle
Some get the marrow bone
And some get nothing
Though there's plenty to spare

from *Banquet* – Joni Mitchell

Meet Eric and Keisha

It was early Saturday morning as Keisha dropped off her twins, Steve, and Dion, at the pool for lessons, then steered her minivan back to her home office. The house was peaceful and quiet as she headed to the kitchen. She made a protein shake, then walked to her office to tackle some paperwork and write her weekly health blog. She hoped to have it all done before her husband, Eric, woke up.

They had met 20 years earlier at Cleveland Browns Stadium as the Browns welcomed (using the term loosely) the Steelers. As luck would have it, Keisha, festooned in orange and brown, was seated next to Eric, clad in black and yellow. At first, the obvious rivalry kept them a bit cool. Eric stole glances at her whenever she was focused on the game. Keisha found herself attracted to him as well, trying to gauge his looks despite his black and yellow face paint. By the start of the third quarter, team loyalties fell, and conversation flowed. Eric mentioned he had recently accepted a job in Cleveland and would be moving next month. Keisha offered him a taste of her nachos and her number. They were engaged a year later.

Now they live on the west side of Cleveland, not far from where Keisha grew up. Despite some obvious friction during football season, they enjoy a good marriage. The twins are doing well in school and show promise on their high school football team. Keisha's blog is gaining in popularity, while Steve's job with an industrial fastener company adds financial stability. They're careful with money and enjoy a comfortable lifestyle.

The hidden problem

Like many Americans, Eric and Keisha's finances are focused on the day-to-day: Paying bills. Making ends meet. Accumulating things that they need—or at least want. They have a nice home, late model cars and can afford programs for their kids, dinners out, and family vacations. While Eric and Keisha have a beautiful family and lots to be thankful for, financially they were setting themselves up for challenges in the future.

Keisha read in a book that people should save at least 10% of their gross income and invest that for the future. Neither of them had a pension and they were saving only about 2% of their incomes. Even that was tough. Each month brought in a dozen or so bills, as well as other expenses like groceries, dinners out, kids' activities, home repairs and pet food. Wanda, their financial advisor, had suggested that with a 2% savings rate,[12] retirement may not be possible until well past age 65. It also meant that they wouldn't be able to realize their dream of taking a year off for an adventure with their kids.

A more immediate issue is that they had no wiggle room in their monthly spend. Pretty much every dollar was allocated. If the roof leaked, the dishwasher quit, or one of the kid's bikes got stolen, they would need to borrow to keep things running.[13] As it was, they were "floating" a few thousand dollars on their credit cards.

They were both aware of these issues but didn't have a good solution. The book that Keisha was reading suggested they set up a detailed budget and pare back on things that they loved. This would free up more money for an emergency fund and a higher savings rate. The problem was that they hated budgeting almost as much as giving up things that they loved. What kind of advice was that?!

But then Keisha noticed something that would change all that. A fresh approach could bring them financial wellness. It all started with a bit of curiosity about a bill.

Broil a bill

Sitting at her desk, Keisha opened an envelope from her car insurance company. Inside was a renewal document showing a premium increase of over 6%. Ouch! Keisha remembered an ad from a car insurance comparison website. Curious, she visited their site and entered information about their vehicles, driving records, and coverage levels. After just ten minutes, she was amazed to see quotes from over a dozen reputable companies, most being much

---

[12] Savings rate is defined as monthly savings divided by monthly income before any deductions or taxes.
[13] Sadly, this isn't unusual, 35% of Americans would struggle to cover a $400 emergency "Report on the Economic Well-Being of U.S. Households in 2020 – May 2021, federalreserve.gov, https://bit.ly/3rbMFIy

less costly than their current rates. She called one of the providers and confirmed the coverage levels and savings of over $200 monthly.[14] Keisha set up the new automatic payment from their joint checking account and cancelled the previous provider.

"Man, I *broiled that bill*," she thought.

She heard moaning and wheezing coming from the kitchen. Husband? Coffee maker? Walking into the kitchen, she saw the final jet of steam as Eric filled his mug. Coffee maker.

"Hopefully, you were able to get enough rest," Keisha said, glancing at her watch as the noon sun highlighted his bed head.

"Could have used a couple more hours, but I'm guessing I'm picking up the twins from swimming," Eric replied, returning her smile, and sipping his joe.

Keisha told him about the car insurance savings. It was unusual to get any kind of good financial news and they pondered ways to spend the good fortune.

"Obviously we should start with landscaping," offered Keisha, "we've talked about that for years."

"Landscaping?!" scoffed Eric, "How about a bigger flatscreen so we can see all the details when the Steelers crush the Browns?"

"How about you start with buying a tank of gas for the van and picking up the kids from swimming?" chuckled Keisha.

Eric grabbed his keys and headed for the door. Keisha returned to her office to finish a blog post. She glanced out her office window to the backyard. The poplars around the perimeter were dying, the deck was looking tired, and the lawn needed re-sodding.

"Landscaping!" she thought.

---

[14] It's also worthwhile to speak with licensed insurance brokers for the best value on car insurance.

Savor the savings

On Monday, as Eric was driving to work, he called Wanda, their financial advisor.

Wanda glanced at the display on her phone. She saw that Eric was calling and expected he might be concerned about the recent market downturn. Each time that happened, her clients would call, wondering if they should sell to avoid market losses.

"Eric! Nice to hear from you. How are Keisha and the twins?"

"All great! How have you been, Wanda?"

"Terrific, thanks. How can I help?"

"Well, I'm a bit concerned about the markets," offered Eric. "Looks like it's down about 8% this week. I'm afraid to peek at my balance online."

"Ha! Markets aren't like a souffle. They won't fall if you open the oven door to look at them. But you are better off looking less! Markets go up and down all the time. It's impossible to time them or to know what they'll do next week. Sometimes news that should move markets up makes them fall and vice versa. The main thing is *time in* the markets, vs. trying to *time the markets*. We have you invested in a quality portfolio of stocks and bonds that will rise *over time*. Stay patient! Look at the growth we have achieved since we began."

Wanda was right. It was the same speech she'd given him many times. There was always a rebound after market dips, and they had averaged 7% annual returns over the last nine years.

"Does that help?" asked Wanda.

"Yeah, I probably just need to hear that every now and again."

"Or, more specifically, after each dip of the market."

They both laughed.

"What else is new with you and Keisha?"

"Well, Keisha found a great way to save us $200 a month on car insurance. We're just thinking through what to do with the freed-up cash."

"What are the options you're considering?"

"Keisha is thinking we should save for landscaping and I'm thinking of a bigger flat screen TV."

"So, this is money that you didn't even know about a week ago?"

"Exactly. She just found this last Saturday."

"So, your yard and TV were fine last week?"

"I guess. What are you suggesting?"

"Well, why not give me the extra $200 a month to invest. Don't just spend it...*savor the savings!*"

"*Savor the savings!* I like that! But that wouldn't make much difference, would it? It's just $200?"

"Remember that it's not $200. *It's $200 a month.* Investing that $200 each month at 7% over 25 years, that's an additional $166,400 when you and Keisha are 65."[15]

"Really? That makes a big difference."

"You bet. A much bigger difference than a new TV or a fancier yard. And remember this *keeps growing.* If you retire at 65, you won't need all that money the day you retire. When you're 75, that money will have grown to $362,400. You'll need cash for that part of your life, as well."

Wanda had given Eric lots to think about. That night, over dinner, they agreed to commit $200 of their insurance savings to additional investments with Wanda.

---

[15] Keep in mind that 64% of Americans will retire with less than $10,000, "64% of Americans Aren't Prepared for Retirement - and 48% Don't Care," gobankingrates.com, September 2019, https://bit.ly/3vo5s4H

Cashflow Cookbook

Here's what this change would free up in monthly cashflow and the extra wealth it would add 25 years later at their planned retirement:

Savings Idea	Extra Monthly Savings	Value at Retirement Invested at 7%
Car insurance	$200	$166,400
Total	$200	$166,400

Turns out, this small tweak would change the way they thought about money and transform their finances more than they could have imagined. And they were just getting started.

Deglaze the debt

A few months later, Eric was at the office when he saw a meeting request from his manager for that afternoon. A bit nerve wracking, since it was unusual for a meeting to be scheduled so suddenly. He grabbed his phone and texted Keisha.

"Just got a new meeting request for this afternoon with Caesar. I'm worried that it's something bad."

"Don't be silly. You're always catastrophizing. It's not like HR will be there as well."

Eric grabbed his mouse and clicked on the meeting. Charmaine from HR *was* invited. A chill ran up his spine.

"Keesh, HR *is* invited."

"Oh, dear. Text me right after."

Eric worked on a proposal until a ding from his computer reminded him it was time to go to Caesar's office. He walked the long hall, his legs feeling a bit drunk, his throat dry. He approached the office and saw Raymond, Caesar's assistant.

"Good afternoon, Eric. Go on in."

Eric tried to read his expression. Upbeat? Concerned? Nothing really. He headed in and greeted Caesar and Charmaine.

"Let me get to the point," began Caesar, "We've been reviewing your performance --"

Eric gulped as a chill ran down his back, along his thighs, and into his knees.

"Nothing short of spectacular! We'd like to offer you our President's Award. A $5,000 bonus and a 7% increase. It will be effective on your next check."

"We're really thrilled for you," said Charmaine, "We'll be announcing this at the next staff meeting."

"Now, get back to work! We need the sales from your desk to keep our revenue rising. Sell some bolts!" laughed Caesar.

They all shook hands and smiled. Eric headed back to his desk and texted Keisha.

"Keesh, it was an award and a raise. Apparently, they like me!"

"Not just them!" Keisha added a heart to her text, then filled his screen with virtual confetti.

Eric drove home, relieved and excited about his news. He pulled into the driveway and the boys rushed out to greet him.

"Does this mean we can go to football camp?" asked Steve.

"And how about new mountain bikes!" added Dion.

"We'll see!" said Keisha. "Your dad and I need to work that all out."

After the boys went to bed, Keisha poured two glasses of Kentucky bourbon for a toast.

"Congratulations! What an accomplishment!" beamed Keisha.

"I'm more relieved than anything else! Does this mean I get my new flat screen TV?" asked Eric.

"I was assuming we could use this money for landscaping!"

They both laughed as they sipped their bourbon.

"Actually, I've been thinking about our debts," Keisha began.

"Like maybe we should use some of this money to pay them down?"

"Is that smarter than investing more with Wanda?"

"Well, we have our mortgage, but it's only at 2.25%."

"True, and our car loans are at low promotional rates. I think they're both below 2%."

"Hmm. I wonder about our credit cards."

Eric opened his iPad and checked the rates on their two cards.

"Looks like they average about 20%."

"Well, we seem to float with a balance of about $6,000 between the two cards. Given the 20% interest rate, we pay about $1,200 a year in interest expense. That's a waste of cash."

"It is for sure, and there is no way that Wanda can get us a consistent return of 20%!" observed Eric.

"Exactly. And that "return" is risk free! So that's like investing in a government bond that pays 20%!" added Keisha.[16]

"OK so we need to get rid of that credit card interest. Stat!" mused Keisha.

After deductions, Eric's bonus was only $3,000, but they used that to pay off the first credit card. They then used $400 of Eric's raise to pay down the second card each month until the balance was zero. Thereafter, they agreed to pay off each card in full each month. With the cards paid off, they saved $100 monthly in interest costs. Paying off the second card freed up another $400. They agreed to send Wanda the combined $500 monthly.

Invested at 7%, that would add another $416,000 to their retirement at age 65.[17] That's an incredible amount of money from

---

[16] Turns out this is an even bigger return, since bond interest is taxable.
[17] This is a big deal and way past the $202,000 that American baby boomers retire with on average, as we learned earlier.

just a couple of small changes. And it even left the rest of the monthly raise to save up for the new TV and the landscaping work. Eric thought about these moves afterward:

We had taken my bonus and put it to work. By paying off that first credit card, we saved the interest cost that was pulling our finances backward. By setting aside part of my raise to pay off that second card, we repeated the process. Then, by committing the $500 to more investments with Wanda, we're pushing our finances forward. Our money is working for us. We really are savoring the savings! At some point, we'll earn more from the rising value of what we own (home and investments) than we will earn from our jobs. We're finally on a path to financial freedom!

Here's the effect on the family's finances after these simple changes:

Savings Idea	Extra Monthly Savings	Value at Retirement Invested at 7%
Car insurance	$200	$166,400
Reduced credit card interest	100	83,200
Savings from raise	400	332,800
Total	$700	$582,400

Eric and Keisha were thrilled with the progress they were making. They'd set out to increase their savings rate and ensure a better retirement and more financial freedom. But they had no idea they would discover even bigger wealth opportunities, all with little effort and minimal sacrifice. But first, they wanted more clarity on their overall financial situation.

Wiser on wealth

It was another Saturday morning, and the twins were enjoying a weekend with their grandparents. Keisha was reading the news on her iPad while relaxing in the sunroom. Eric came out to join her, bringing a tray of coffee and muffins.

"I've been thinking about our financial moves. It seems like they're really making a difference for our future. And it's all so simple to do!" said Keisha.

"Yes, but I've been wondering about the overall picture. Our accounts with Wanda are growing, but we have our house and mortgage, car loans, my company stock plan, and the value of your blog. Are we getting ahead, or falling behind?"

Eric pulled out his laptop and their financial records. He set up a simple spreadsheet. In the first column, he put the heading **Owned,** and under that he listed house, vehicles, their accounts with Wanda, Eric's 401(k), and the value of Keisha's blog business. Below that was the heading **Owed**, where Eric listed their mortgage, vehicle loans, and credit card debts. Just below that was a **Wealth** heading, indicating everything they *owned* minus everything they *owed*. Across the top were years, starting with the current one and going out five years.

To get values for what they own, Keisha checked with real estate sites to estimate the value of their home and used car listings for the current value of their vehicles. For their investments, Eric checked the figures from the financial plan that Wanda had prepared. They estimated the value of Keisha's blog. To get the value of what they owe, they checked mortgage and car loan statements. After about an hour's work, they had the current year completed, then started filling in the future years by estimating growth rates in real estate for their house, investment gains using projections from Wanda, and Keisha's business plan for blog growth.

When the spreadsheet was done, they were pleased to see their overall wealth was growing over time. They could see the value of their home and investments increasing, while of value of their vehicles, as well as mortgage and car loan balances decreased over time. It was great to see it all in one place. They were getting *wiser on their wealth*. A simplified version of their spreadsheet looks like this:[18]

Eric & Keisha Wealth Tracker

Owned	2022	2023	2024	2025	2026
House	450,000	472,500	496,125	520,931	546,977
Minivan	28,000	25,200	22,680	20,412	18,371
SUV	36,000	32,400	29,160	26,244	23,619
Investments	128,000	149,158	171,797	196,020	221,940
Total Owned	642,000	679,258	719,762	763,607	810,907
Owed	**2022**	**2023**	**2024**	**2025**	**2026**
Mortgage	374,000	366,609	349,811	341,053	332,047
Minivan Loan	21,500	15,879	10,560	5111	0
SUV Loan	28,262	20,873	13,881	6718	0
Credit Card 1	3,000	0	0	0	0
Credit Card 2	3,000	0	0	0	0
Total Owed	429,762	403,361	374,252	352,882	332,047
Wealth	**212,238**	**275,897**	**345,510**	**410,725**	**478,860**
Wealth Increase		+63,659	+69,613	+65,215	+68,135

Eric stared at the chart. Starting on the **Total Owned** *line, he was amazed to see that what they owned would rise by about $170,000 over just five years. Those extra contributions to Wanda would really help! And their* **Total Owed** *would drop by nearly $100,000. Paying off those credit cards helped there! Looking at the* **Wealth** *row near the bottom, their total wealth would more than double in just 5 years. Incredible. The bottom row showed the change*

---

[18] To build your own Wealth spreadsheet, download the free template in the **Utensils** section at CashflowCookbook.com.

in wealth from one year to the next. Updating this tracker on a regular basis will help the couple adopt a wealth mindset and change the way they think about money.

They both went to bed pondering what other changes they could make to accelerate the growth of their wealth. Building that wealth would give them options: more financial security, increased charitable contributions, a chance at a sabbatical year or two, extra money for college for the boys, or just peace of mind for their retirement. Maybe even total financial freedom and a chance to live life on their own terms.

Eric and Keisha didn't know all those options were about to become viable and that they would be able to do this with little effort, minimal sacrifice, and no extra risk. But first, they had a new issue to fix.

Beautify the banking

It was the 27th of the month when Eric dropped by Best Buy after work to get a new phone. He opened his banking app and saw there was a healthy balance in their joint account. Eric went ahead with the purchase, then headed out to a sports bar to watch football with friends.

The next morning, Keisha was having lunch at her desk, reviewing her web traffic stats when her phone rang.

"Keisha, it's Marcia from the bank. How's your day going?"

"The morning has been great, "offered Keisha, "but I'm concerned that might be about to change."

"Well, I was calling about your mortgage refinancing papers, they're complete and ready for pick up. But I did notice that your joint checking account is overdrawn."

"Ugh! How did that happen? So embarrassing."

"Well, it looks like your automated mortgage payment went through, but that left your T-Mobile payment wanting."

"Hmm, like wanting for more cash?"

"Yes. And, unfortunately, I'm unable to waive the overdraft fee, as I've done the last few times."

Ouch.

"Got it Marcia, thanks for the call."

Keisha spent an hour moving money around, calling T-Mobile and straightening everything out. It appeared that the culprit was a Best Buy purchase that must have been made by Eric.

That night, after dinner, Keisha raised the issue with her husband.

"Marcia called me from the bank today. Looks like we're overdrawn again. Did you get something at Best Buy yesterday?"

"Oh, yeah, my new iPhone. We spoke about that earlier."

"Well, our mortgage payment and T-Mobile account both come out on the 28th of the month, meaning the phone purchase left us overdrawn."

"I'm sorry. I checked the account, but I forgot about those automated payments. We need to find a better way to handle this."

Keisha and Eric spent time sketching out new ideas to manage their cashflow and avoid overdrafts. They looked at keeping a list of automated bill payments and the dates they would be paid. They then considered weekly meetings to see what bills are coming and what personal things are needed. Both ideas were as appealing as a bag of takeout sushi forgotten in the car overnight. In July.

"It strikes me that the issue is the mix of these automated payments with our day-to-day expenses, such as groceries, dinners out, and personal items. Why don't we just use one checking account to pay all the recurring bills and another for day-to-day things?" offered Keisha.

"I actually had that same idea," said Eric winking.

Keisha booked time with Marcia at the bank, who set up monthly automatic transfers, sending a fixed amount to the new "bill account" to more than cover the payments, with the rest left in their joint account.

"I'll miss our phone calls," said Marcia with a grin.

"I won't!" laughed Keisha.

Beautifying their banking would end the overdraft fees and marital financial stress. But having all the monthly bills in one place sparked a new idea that would lead the couple to even bigger wealth accelerators.

Broil a bunch of bills

It was an early Sunday morning and Keisha was in her home office, reviewing the transactions in their recurring bills account. As she scanned the list, she was pleased to see the reduction in car insurance payments. Incredible that just a few minutes of her time had led to that $200 monthly savings, and, more importantly, the extra $166,400 it would mean for them at retirement. Then it hit her with all the subtlety of a burnt pot roast. Car insurance was just one bill. Might there be opportunities in all the other little monthly monsters?

Using the withdrawal activity, she made a list of all their recurring bills:

Regular Monthly Bills	Amount
Mortgage	$1,750
Property taxes	$283
Home insurance	$227
Natural gas	$143
Electricity	$187

Regular Monthly Bills	Amount
Water/Sewer	$102
Internet/TV/Phone	$260
Netflix	$14
Minivan loan	$420
SUV loan	$587
Car insurance	$124
Eric's satellite radio	$12
Dion's piano lessons	$200
Gym memberships	$62
Life insurance (Keisha)	$120
Cell phones (4)	$210
Total	**$4,701**

This hit Keisha like the smell of a forgotten fridge leftover. If she found $200 in just one bill, what kind of savings might result by lowering all of them? And by investing those monthly savings with Wanda, they could really accelerate their wealth. Maybe they could even…

Keisha heard Eric in the kitchen and called him to her office.

"Eric, I'm looking at all these monthly bills. Why don't we *broil a bunch of bills*? It worked so well for our car insurance, why stop there?"

Eric peered at the printed list.

"Hmm, I have a satellite radio plan in my SUV? I didn't know that! I usually just listen to podcasts." pondered Eric

"Well, I guess you won't miss it then!" smiled Keisha as she shaded it with a yellow highlighter.

"Our gym memberships are about 5x that amount. What if we replace them with an online fitness app and work out on that spinning bike that holds laundry in the basement?

Cashflow Cookbook

"How about I take the top half of the list and you take the bottom? Let's check back in two weeks and see who has saved what."

"It's a plan!" Keisha exclaimed. "I'll send us a calendar invite for two weeks from today. Shall we do a Zoom or meet at the kitchen table?"

"Let's meet in person, I look too washed out on Zoom," Eric laughed and headed out to shoot hoops with the boys.

Over the next couple of weeks, they each worked on their set of bills. Some decisions were easy, and they were able to act on them individually; others would need to be considered between the two of them. Some were about conserving usage including natural gas, electricity, and water/sewer. Others were about changing the paradigm on expenses like internet/tv/phone, video streaming services, satellite radio, piano lessons, and gym memberships. Many were about comparison shopping, including using online tools to rapidly compare vendors. And still others were about ways to lower costs from a sole supplier, like property taxes. Through their research, they were surprised to find that *ALL their bills could be lowered.*[19]

At the agreed time, they met at the kitchen table. Keisha saw that Eric had laid out a brunch spread and a pot of fresh brewed coffee.

"Wow! A bit extravagant," said Keisha, smiling at the rich bounty. "Can we afford this?"

"We can with the savings I found! Let's get right to it. Do you want to start?"

"Sure. I cancelled your satellite radio for an easy $12."

---

[19] For more detailed information on reducing costs of recurring expenses, go to Part 2 of this book, as well as cashflowcookbook.com. The **Blog** posts include complete examples of savings, The **Utensils** section has worksheets and negotiating scripts, while the **Ingredients** section has links to providers that can reduce just about any expense.

"Nice opening," offered Eric, downing a mini quiche.

"Then I reviewed our car loans. Both were at low promotional rates. One is at 1.25% and the other is at 1.5%, so there's no logic renegotiating them. On the good news front, I found an online piano teacher who comes very highly rated. Dion says that he is up for trying that, which could save us another $180. I'm going to switch our gym to online classes, saving $42.[20] I found a life insurance comparison tool and will be switching to a reputable term life provider to save another $36. Then I called our cell phone company. When I told them I was concerned about our bill and considering other providers, they got us on a better plan, saving us another $37.[21] Grand total of $307 monthly."

"Impressive!" Eric smiled, "Not bad for two weeks of work!"

"Actually, the whole thing took about three hours! So that's like earning over $100 an hour."

Eric opened his laptop and did some future value calculations.

"If we invested the $307 at 7% for the next 40 years, that would give us an extra $804,647. Dividing that by the three hours of work you did, means that you were working for $268,215 an hour!"

"OK, that's a lot more than I make with my blog! Over to you, my friend, what did you find?"

"Well!" said Eric, "I started with the mortgage, which we just refinanced, so no action there. The property taxes can be appealed in our area, so I'm gathering the necessary information. My friend, Miguel, had his lowered by $125 a month, so it's worth a try. The comparison site you found for car insurance also offers home insurance, so switching and combining the two with the same vendor can save us another $85."

---

[20] For providers of comparison tools, online music lessons, virtual gyms and lots more, refer to the **Ingredients** section of CashflowCookbook.com.
[21] See the **Utilities** section of cashflowcookbook.com for a sample script to use while calling your cell phone provider to negotiate better rates.

Eric took a spoonful of his breakfast parfait and moved on.

"I found that our gas company does complete home energy audits for a nominal fee, which can pinpoint how we can save energy. I booked them for the 22nd. In the meanwhile, I bought twenty LED light bulbs to replace the ones we use most, which should save us $20. There's a much bigger opportunity in home entertainment. Between Internet, TV, home phone and Netflix, we spend $274 a month. But we rarely watch regular TV. And we never use our home phone. I found an app that can get us sports and most TV channels. Using that app, an internet plan, and Netflix would save us $135. So, my total is $240—not including lower energy costs and reduced taxes."

He set his spoon down and took a big slurp of his coffee.

"Love this," said Keisha, "so together, we've found $547 with more to come!"

Making these changes offered other possibilities as well: money for college, a chance to retire earlier, more cash for charity contributions, and the ability to create an emergency fund.

The couple spent the next couple of weeks making all the changes to their bills. They decided to commit an additional $500 to their monthly contributions with Wanda, and the remaining $47 to an emergency fund. Their extra savings and additional wealth at retirement now looked like this:

Savings Idea	Extra Monthly Savings	Value at Retirement Invested at 7%
Car insurance	$200	$166,400
Credit card interest	100	83,200
Savings from raise	400	332,800
Savings from bill reduction	500	416,000
Total	$1,200	$998,400

Although they'd made tremendous strides on their finances, there was still one major area that would provide them with even more financial wellness.

Dice the discretionary

Eric and Keisha liked to tackle home projects on Sunday afternoons. This week they decided to focus on decluttering their clothes closets. They'd already worked with the boys to purge their clothes and gathered a garbage bag and a half. Now they were running a fashion show for each other to make piles of keep, maybe, and what-were-we-thinking? The latter provided the most entertainment.

"Did you buy that when you were nine?" laughed Keisha as Eric tried on a faded blue t-shirt that failed to cover his navel.

"I just got this a few years ago!" smiled Eric, tugging it down.

They worked through the rest of Eric's clothes, yielding a garbage bag and a half. Then, it was Keisha's turn.

"The crossing guard called. He wants his vest back." Eric laughed as Keisha tried on an orange vest that was two sizes too big.

"But I got it on sale! It's a good brand." Keisha smiled.

"I wonder why such a thing would go on sale?" asked Eric.

In total, they gathered five garbage bags of clothing. They muscled them down to the car and loaded everything into the trunk and headed to the drop off box.

"We really need to do this more often," said Eric.

"We just did this one year ago, remember? It was your aunt's birthday," said Keisha.

"I can't believe this is just one year's waste," Eric replied.

They pondered the money that they had squandered on clothing. Mostly clothing they had *never* even worn.

"Let's say that each bag holds twenty items," Keisha began.

"Hmm and about $40 per item?" offered Eric.

"Yep, so that is $800 per bag and five bags. Could we have wasted $4,000 on clothing in a year?" Keisha was shocked.

"It seems like there are big opportunities to save in day-to-day spending, as well as the monthly bills," offered Eric," I'm thinking we need to *dice the discretionary.*"

They pulled out a sheet of paper and a pen, and noted categories that were outside the usual recurring monthly bills, focusing on a handful of items:

- Dining out
- Groceries
- Clothing
- Prescription drugs

"Well, I think we can commit to shopping more mindfully for clothing," began Eric, "How about we make a rule that we do our clothing shopping when we really need a specific piece?"

"And check first to see if there already is one somewhere in the back of the closet!" added Keisha.

"We've already done the math on this one. We know we wasted $4,000 in the last year. Let's be conservative. Is it reasonable that we can save $150 a month by shopping more mindfully?" asked Eric.

"I think so," said Keisha, "that's less than half of what we wasted last year!"

They then looked at their monthly grocery bill. With two teenage boys it routinely ran into four digits. They talked about clipping coupons and driving to different grocery stores, but it seemed like a lot of work. Chasing cheap cereal in the west and discounted dairy in the east. Ugh.

"I was chatting with our neighbor Bob about his free grocery store loyalty card. He and James are empty nesters, but they saved

$1,250 in the last twelve months. He showed me his last receipt. It had a running total at the bottom," offered Keisha.

"Wow, if they are saving over $100 monthly with just the two of them, we would easily save $150 with the four of us," said Eric.

Keisha noted the grocery savings at $150, and the clothing savings, at another $150 monthly. She made a note to sign up for the grocery loyalty program.

"OK, well, thinking about dining out, I have to say that I buy lunch pretty much every day. Looking at our debit card charges, that averages about $15 a day. With twenty-one working days in a month, that's over $300." said Eric.

"Why not bring ten lunches a month?" offered Keisha, "That would easily save $100 and probably be healthier."

Keisha committed the amount to the worksheet. Eric smiled and thought better of objecting. They'd now freed up $400 monthly—all with little effort or sacrifice.

"I'm looking at your prescription meds," said Eric. "They're about $120 each month. What about an online pharmacy? Might that be cheaper?"

Keisha opened her laptop and found an accredited online pharmacy that looked promising. She entered her meds and the dosage and was shocked to find them available for only $12 monthly, delivered right to her door.[22] She spun the laptop toward Eric and added another $100 to her worksheet.

"Let me throw out one more idea. We go out for family dinners once a week. If you and I shared an appetizer and a desert, that would save about $25 per meal, or over $100 a month. Same dinner, same fun. And we save a few calories. What do you think?" asked Keisha.

---

[22] For links to low-cost online pharmacies, refer to the **Ingredients** section of CashflowCookbook.com

"That sounds like an easy change to make."

Keisha noted it on her worksheet. The total savings from their daily spend account was a remarkable $600 monthly. All for giving up clothing they would never wear, a few calories they could do without and making ten lunches a month—and having their pills delivered by mail rather than driving to get them at a pharmacy.

"It's interesting. As we look at all these day-to-day expenses, it seems to me that this is about being more mindful—taking a minute to look at each item and category before buying. In my mind, I now have a *check list* before pulling out my *check book*:"

- Do we need it?
- Can we borrow it?
- Can we rent it?
- Can we get a used one?
- Can we shop for a better price?
- Is there a better way to buy this type of thing?
- Is there a way to get it at a discount?
- Can we substitute with something else?

"I like that! I can't believe how easy all of this was," said Eric, "We did it all with minimal effort, little sacrifice, and no budgeting. Now, we just need to automate sending this cash to Wanda each month so she can invest it for us. And as we find new savings or income, we can commit part to savings and keep part for fun money."

"Like our landscaping?" laughed Keisha.

"I was at Best Buy today. They don't do landscaping." deadpanned Eric.

"Nice try." said Keisha.

Here's a summary of the changes Eric and Keisha made:

Savings Idea	Extra Monthly Savings	Value at Retirement Invested at 7%
Car insurance	$200	$166,400
Credit card interest	100	83,200
Savings from raise	400	332,800
Savings from bill reduction	500	416,000
Savings from daily spending	600	499,200
Total	$1,800	$1,497,600

They were able to free up a total of $1,800 monthly they would invest through their financial advisor. If they could average 7% annual growth on their investments, this would give them nearly one and a half million dollars of additional wealth at their retirement. They were able to get these results with *just a handful of easy changes*. What if they looked at 60 more ideas that provide over $13,000 of monthly savings ideas with the potential to add more than $2 million in wealth over ten years? That's exactly what they'll do in **Part II – The Recipes**. But first, let's look at the **Takeout Container** to see how much they saved from this initial exercise.

The takeout container

Eric and Keisha are like many Americans. They're working hard and providing for their family, but not building financial freedom. They don't have flexibility to retire early, take a year off or increase their charitable contributions. More important, a small financial calamity, such as a broken dishwasher, a leaky roof, or a plumbing backup could lead to more debt.

They discovered a different way of thinking about their money and made simple changes that set them on a path to financial wellness. They're just starting, and they'll find dozens more ideas in the financial recipes ahead.

Here are some thoughts from this section:

- **Broil a Bill** – Lowering a recurring monthly bill is a great place to start to improve your finances. All bills can be lowered by eliminating unused services, using less, renegotiating, comparing providers, or switching to a disruptive service. Always check out the reputation and credentials of the new provider. Try it once, you'll be hungry for more!

- **Savor the Savings** – Once you free up cashflow, put it to good use by paying down debt, increasing investment, increasing an emergency fund, or using a part of it for charity or fun. Be conscious about this to really see the value. Everyone's situation is different. Assess which use of the freed-up cashflow is most important to your situation.

- **Deglaze the Debt** – High interest debt paydown is a priority. Generally, the most important debt to pay off is credit card debt, and then to continue to pay the cards in full each month. After that, assess whether debt paydown is a higher priority than more investments. Every situation is different. For Eric and Keisha, their credit card debt was clearly the place to start. Check with your accountant or financial planner for your situation.

- **Wiser on Wealth** – Wealth is the difference of what you own minus what you owe. Having wealth gives you options: a year off, early retirement, handling an emergency, switching to a more meaningful career, or starting a small business. Tracking wealth helps you visualize your progress and makes you think differently about how you spend. You may want to track this monthly for a year to build your awareness, then quarterly or yearly after that.

- **Beautify the Banking** – Having a separate account for day-to-day banking vs bill payment has two benefits:
  - It makes money management easier since it reduces overdrafts and "surprises."
  - It adds focus on the recuring monthly bills that can be reduced.
- **Broil a Bunch of Bills** – Once you find savings on your first monthly bill, make a list and work on all of them. Calculate how much you can save from each, then apply the savings to debt reduction, extra investment, or an emergency fund—depending on your situation.
- **Dice the Discretionary** – Our discretionary spending can also be reduced with minimal effort or sacrifice. A simple set of questions can help us shop more mindfully: Do we need it? Can we borrow it? Can we rent it? Can we get a used one? Can we shop for a better price? Can we substitute with something else? Shopping more mindfully can slash our costs with minimal impact to our lifestyle.

Q&A with the chef

Having spoken on Cashflow Cookbook at conferences, to financial advisors and their clients, associations, employee groups, and students in both the US and Canada, I've learned there are a consistent set of questions that come up about the approach. Let's look at those now, before we head to the kitchen to sample more recipes.

Q: *It's great that Eric and Keisha don't have very much debt. We still have student loans as well as a big mortgage, a line of credit, and plenty of credit card debt.*

A: Everyone's situation is different. If your main issue is debt, consider using the freed up cashflow to pay that down. Focus on the highest interest rate loans first, pay them off, then go to the next highest rate loans. Or, you can pay off the smallest loans and use that cash to pay down the next largest loan.

Your situation is actually very similar to Eric and Keisha in that you're both using freed-up cashflow to increase your overall wealth. Whether it's applied to debt or more investments, it's building your wealth. If you have significant high interest debt, these ideas become even more powerful. Be sure to track your wealth each month, just like Eric and Keisha. As you pay down that debt, you'll be able to watch your wealth grow on your wealth sheet.

Q: *We tried to track our wealth, but the actual number is negative! We found out that we owe more than we own. I guess this won't work for us.*

A: Actually, it *will* work well for you. The idea is to increase your wealth. If you have negative wealth now, then look for ways to free up cashflow to pay down your debts faster. As you pay down those debts, you will be paying less interest each year and the balance will continue to drop. When you're left with just low interest rate debt, you can shift your focus to building assets and investing.

Q: *There's no way I can earn 7% investing! My bank only pays 0.5% interest on deposits.*

A: Correct. You can't get any kind of decent return from bank deposits. To earn a real return, you'll need to invest in stocks and bonds of solid, well managed companies over a long period of time. As an example, the S&P 500 (a benchmark of the US stock market) has delivered an average return of 10.5%.[23] That includes during wars, presidential elections, 9/11, and COVID-19. Your results will vary from year to year. A competent financial advisor will set up a portfolio that suits your situation, age, stage, and risk preferences. If you like, you can plan with a different growth rate for your investments.

You could also invest in real estate, rare art, your own business, whole life insurance policies, vintage cars, or cryptocurrency. Each has their own risks and rewards. Do your own research and consult a qualified investment professional to choose the right investment for you.

Q: *The changes that Eric and Keisha made don't apply to my situation or aren't realistic.*

A: Everyone is different. You may not receive a raise, your prescription drugs may be fully covered by your health care plan, or perhaps you have no car. Gotcha! But you likely live somewhere, buy food, pay for transportation, and have a cell phone or five in your family. All those costs may be reduced. In **Part II – The Recipes**, you'll find dozens of recipes to free up cashflow. At least a few will work for you.

Q: *I'm too young (or too old) to make any of this work.*
A: I don't think so!

If you're in your teens, now is a great time to learn the concepts in the book. Work with your parents and help them to free up more cashflow to invest or pay down debt.

If you're in your 20's, you're starting to get bills. Learn how to reduce them and track your wealth each year, even if it's negative.

---

[23] "What is the Average Annual Return for the S&P 500?" Investopedia.com, January 2022, https://bit.ly/3jlt2ta

Each dollar that you invest at 25 will be worth $16 when you're 65 (which sounds like forever, I know!). Build the mindset.

If you're in your 30's and 40's, you still have lots of time to see dramatic growth through compounding. You're also in peak spending years, setting up your home, and perhaps raising kids. Lots of bills and expenses to optimize.

In your 50's and 60's, you still may have another 30 or 40 years of life ahead and some of your money will be invested until then.

If you're retired, these ideas can reduce your "burn rate" and slow spending of your savings.

Pick what goes on your financial plate.

Wrapping up Part 1

By now you get the idea. Some of what just worked for Eric and Keisha will be easy for you to implement. Other ideas may not apply. But the plan remains the same: Find ways to reduce your costs with minimal effort or sacrifice. Get that monthly cashflow working for you by paying down debt or increasing your investment in solid, safe growth opportunities.

You're ready for **Part 2 – The Recipes**. In this section, we'll look at dozens of different financial "recipes" that free up cashflow. Lots of cashflow. In fact, all the recipes together could free up more than $13,000 monthly. Yes, *monthly*. Not everything will work for you. But might you be able to find $500, $1,000 or $2,000 per month?

Download the Wealth Tracker template from cashflowcookbook.com and let's find out!

Part 2 – The Recipes

"I love money. I love everything about it. I bought some pretty good stuff. Got me a $300 pair of socks. Got a fur sink. An electric dog polisher. A gasoline powered turtleneck sweater. And, of course, I bought some dumb stuff, too."

— Steve Martin

How to use this section

If you built a *Wealth Tracker* like Eric and Keisha, you now have a sense of the state of your financial kitchen. If you didn't, take a moment now and build one. You've started to scrutinize your bills and look for ways to reduce them to free up cashflow. If you have high-interest debts, you know that using that extra cashflow to pay those off is a priority. If you have only low-interest debt, you may want to focus on increasing your investments. If this decision is complicated and you aren't sure where to best apply your new cashflow, consult with an accountant or qualified financial professional. *Remember: We're offering recommendations, but your personal situation may require different actions.*

The recipes are divided into six sections: housing, transportation, food & drink, household, lifestyle, and financial. Each section includes ten recipes. They start with smaller savings ideas and work up to larger ones.

Each recipe includes ideas for reducing that expense category. As you look through these you may feel the savings aren't realistic for you. Namaste. That's why there's a place for you to do your *own* math for each recipe. You may find that some don't apply to you. No problem. Flip ahead to the next recipe. At the end of each section is a **Takeout Container** that summarizes the recipes in that part of the book.

> If you are making any changes based on the recipes, always do your diligence prior to acting. This book offers ideas on ways to save. See if they're a fit, do your own research, and get professional help as needed.

Important: As you work through the recipes, immediately **Savor the Savings** to pay down debt, increase your savings, or start an emergency fund. Set up or increase automated transfers right away. Don't just let the money stew in your checking account or someone will slurp it away. (I think you know who you are.)

Just before we roll up our sleeves and start spattering ingredients around, here are a few more details on how to use the recipes. Just under the title, you will see some symbols:

$ More dollar signs mean a recipe offers more savings.

Y   More whisks mean more effort will be required to put the recipe into action.

⏳   An egg timer means the savings will be longer-term.

Each recipe includes suggested ingredients or ways to realize the savings. In many cases, you might benefit from the services of a company. For example, there are websites that allow you to compare costs of insurance, review lower-cost vendors for products, or discover innovative firms that disrupt established competitors. Some possible companies and their websites are included in the **Ingredients** section on CashflowCookbook.com. Keep your web-connected device handy as you do your financial cookin'.

> Some of the recipes include **Pro Chef Tips**: extra ideas to keep you safe, free up more cashflow, or make the recipe easier.

At the end of each recipe is a **Yield Table**. The examples show how much you would save if you invested your monthly savings with a 7% return. Why 7%? It's a reasonable estimate of what you might earn on your investments. It can also represent the interest rate on loans you wish to repay.

To help you get started on serving up the savings, each recipe describes an example of a **Hearty Serving**, which shows the larger impact of the recipe on a medium or large family with multiple cars, houses, and/or kids. Below that is an example of a **Light Serving**, showing the impact of the recipe on a single person or a small family with less stuff. These show you a range of what savings might look like. Note that all of the calculations are based on monthly amounts. Annual amounts are converted to monthly in the calculations.

The columns in the **Yield Table** show the kind of savings the recipe offers, then what those monthly savings might amount to if invested for ten, twenty, or thirty years. For the **10-year value,** simply multiply your monthly savings by 173. For the **20-year value**, multiply the monthly savings by 52. Multiply by 1,226 for the **30-year value.**[24]

---

[24] The 10-, 20-, and 30-year values assume that you can invest your freed up monthly cashflow at 7%. To see the multiplying factors for other interest rates or for longer periods of time, refer to the Utilities section of CashflowCookbook.com

Below the two example rows in the yield table is a row for **your info**. This is where you can do your own math to estimate your savings. Just plug in your monthly savings numbers and multiply them by 173, 521, and 1,226 as in the examples. That will show you how much the monthly savings might grow to over ten, twenty, or thirty years. It's that easy!

Remember that the light and hearty servings are just examples. Use the ideas listed under **Ingredients** and tweak the recipes to suit your taste—there's no reason to treat them as cookie cutters.[25]

Although the recipes only show the math for ten, twenty, and thirty years, the savings become truly massive at forty years, which sounds like an awfully long time. But if you're 25 and intend to work till 65, that's forty years. If you could use just one recipe that saves, say, $200 monthly, invest that money, and earn 7% over your 40-year career, you would have $524,800 at retirement. *Just from one recipe!* Yum!

After you calculate your savings for each recipe, remember to increase your monthly debt payments, investment contributions or emergency savings by that amount. And, yes, maybe leave some cash in your checking account for fun things. Be sure to update your **Wealth Tracker** so that you can see growth in the value of what you own, a decline in what you owe, and track how your wealth is growing over time.

Come back and revisit the recipes in the years to come to find new savings ideas as your lifestyle changes. Bon appétit.

---

[25] Kindly allow me to offer a general apology in advance for all the cooking puns. Hope you'll find them tasty.

Cashflow Cookbook

Housing

HOUSING COSTS TAKE UP 30% of the average US household budget,[26] making them the biggest single expense category. Let's put them on a diet.

Some of these recipes will work even if you are renting, but all of them can take a bite out of your expenses if you own a house or condo.

Every home expense presents an opportunity for savings, so let's get out the grater and start shaving them all down to size. We'll look at the dollar costs of:

- Alarms: Maybe it's not just the burglar ripping you off
- Insurance: Coverage and rates
- Utilities: Gas and electricity
- Financing: Mortgage costs
- Contents: Art, furniture, carpets, drapes, appliances
- Repairs: Regular repairs and maintenance

And lots more.

Let's start with some of the smaller recipes and work our way up to the advanced dishes.

---

[26] Karen Bennett, "What Americans spend: A look at the cost of housing, food, transportation and more," Bankrate.com, January 2022, https://bit.ly/3Ji36Jm

Hashed Home Alarm

 $

Being safe and secure in your home is as comforting as a big plate of Shepherd's Pie, but the monthly monitoring cost may leave a bad taste in your mouth. Protecting your home is important and it can save on insurance premiums, but you may not need all the trimmings.

Let's cook up some savings! If you've had your system in place for some time, you are likely now "out of contract," meaning you own the actual alarm gear and may be free to move the monitoring of the system to a lower-cost provider. If you don't have a system, your options are even broader. Shop around!

No home alarm or plan to get one? Move on to the next recipe.

Ingredients

- If you're about to get an alarm, be sure to compare multiple providers and read consumer reviews.
- If you have an existing system, review your contract, or call your provider to see if you are still under contract.
- Are you paying for alarm features that you don't need?
- Can you replace your existing monitoring with a reputable discount alarm monitoring firm that will work with your hardware?
- Are you paying for a landline that you only use for your home alarm? Some options save the expense of a dedicated landline.
- Ask your existing company and some of the discount monitoring firms for their best quotes.
- Go bake your best deal!

Hearty Serving

- Two properties
- Two monitored alarms at $40 = $80 monthly
- Switch to reputable discount monitoring at $10 each
- New cost: $20 monthly
- Savings: $60 monthly

Light Serving

- One home
- Monitored alarm costing $35 monthly
- Switch to reputable discount monitoring at $10
- New cost: $10
- Savings: $25 monthly

Yield

Servings	Monthly Savings	10-Year × 173	20-Year × 521	30-Year × 1226
Hearty	$60	$10,380	$31,260	$73,560
Light	$25	$4,325	$13,025	$30,650
Your info				

Add your data to the table above, lock the freed-up cash into debt reduction or increased savings and you're on to the next recipe. Keep track of your total savings as you complete each recipe.

Steeped Snow Blowing

$ ¶¶¶

If you have a pricey snow removal service coming to your home to clear your driveway and sidewalk, you may be blowing cash as well as snow.

Plowing services face a challenge: The heavier the snowfall, the busier their day. This means on the days you most need them, they're often late digging you out. That's about as useful as stirring the chili *after* it's a burnt mass welded to the bottom of the pot.

Let's chop some excess costs and get great service.

Ingredients

- If you don't have much of a driveway, set down the remote and if you are able, rise from the couch and start shovelling!

- Too much work? Not able to do this yourself? Find a dependable local teenager to do it. Perhaps you even raised one yourself. Time for them to get to work!

- If you have a disability or you're over 65, you may be eligible for free snow removal service. Check with your municipality.

- Check out the Uber-like on-demand snow removal apps that are available in your area and see if their rates are better than the local snow removal crews.[27]

- If you have a big driveway, why not find a neighbor, and go halves on a used snow blower? Odd days of the month, you do the work; even days, she covers it.

---

[27] Check under Housing in the Ingredients Section of CashflowCookbook.com for snow removal apps.

- Shop online for used snow blowers. Check for clean oil on the dipstick. Does the machine look like it's been well cared-for? Start it up and give it a test drive. If necessary, take a mechanically minded friend to give it the once-over. Shop in the spring for the best deals on new and used blowers.

Hearty Serving
- Two neighboring households with large driveways
- Each paying equivalent of $67 monthly for snow plowing
- Split the cost of a large used snow blower: $600 each
- New cost over 48-month lifespan: $7 monthly, including some do-it-yourself maintenance
- Savings: $60 monthly

Light Serving
- Two neighboring households with small driveways
- Each paying equivalent of $33 monthly for snow plowing
- Split the cost of a small used snow blower, $400 each
- New cost over 48-month lifespan: $5 monthly, including some do-it-yourself maintenance
- Savings: $29 monthly

Yield

Servings	Monthly Savings	10-Year × 173	20-Year × 521	30-Year × 1226
Hearty	$60	$10,380	$31,260	$73,560
Light	$29	$5,017	$15,109	$35,554
Your info				

Great savings, fresh air, exercise, and self-sufficiency. And only you and your neighbor to blame if the job isn't done on time! Yes, it works for grass cutting too!

Heated Home Insurance

$

Coming home to a pile of smoking ash where your house used to stand isn't fun. But having hundreds of dollars in insurance premiums singe your checking account each month isn't attractive either.

Many of us ignore our home insurance costs since they are often paid by our mortgage lender along with our house taxes and the actual mortgage payment. Ignore no more.

In the olden days, finding savings on home insurance involved calling around, listening to bad hold music, and having to slowly spell your surname to a voice robot several times. Nowadays, there are insurance comparison engines that let you do this on the web in minutes while matching coverage (liability, limits, and deductibles).[28]

Ingredients

- Use the online comparison tools to evaluate providers and/or work with a licensed independent insurance broker.
- Don't over-insure—gather information on the actual value of your lot and contents, and the cost of rebuilding your house.
- Aim for the highest deductible you can reasonably afford.
- Look at bundling home and car insurance with one company.
- Take advantage of all possible discounts: home alarms, updated wiring, proximity to fire hydrants, freshly decorated, etc.[29]
- Compare the total cost of paying monthly vs. annually—it can be 5% cheaper to pay annually.

---

[28] For home insurance comparison sites, see Housing within the Ingredients section at CashflowCookbook.com.
[29] Worth a try.

       Cashflow Cookbook

Hearty Serving

- Large home and a vacation property
- Total insurance cost of $312 monthly
- Combine home and auto coverage, switch to a cheaper provider, align coverage with value of home and contents
- New insurance cost: $225 monthly
- Savings: $87 monthly

Light Serving

- One smaller home
- Insurance cost of $150 monthly
- Combine home and auto coverage, raise deductible, switch to annual payments from monthly
- New insurance cost: $117 monthly
- Savings: $33 monthly

Yield

Servings	Monthly Savings	10-Year × 173	20-Year × 521	30-Year × 1226
Hearty	$87	$15,051	$45,327	$106,662
Light	$33	$5,709	$17,193	$40,458
Your info				

Imagine yourself, twenty years from now, wondering whether you should have invested an hour today to add over $100,000 dollars or so to your wealth at retirement!

Tandooried Taxes

$ $ 🍸

Property taxes are one of those things that seem hard to lose—like those last ten pounds, or the neighbor who can't stay long and just dropped by for a quick chat. Unfortunately, unlike either of those, there's no way to make your taxes vanish, but you can reduce them.

Nationally, 30-60% of people overpay on their property taxes, yet only 5% appeal.[30] There may also be other ways to lower your taxes without an appeal. Let's start by understanding how your taxes are calculated, then we'll season in some savings.

Taxes are calculated as an assessed value of your home multiplied by a local factor called a *mill rate*. Your assessed value is the number that needs attention. You'll find a summary of this information on your tax bill and more detailed information is available at your municipal tax office, or online in some cases.

Ingredients

- Pursue an appeal of your assessed value, which involves building a case that your assessment is too high due to incorrect information about your lot or dwelling, or that it's overvalued relative to other homes in the neighborhood. Information on comparable homes can be gathered through real estate sites, your agent, or your county tax web site. Or hire a property tax expert.
- If you qualify, pursue one of these Homestead Exemptions:
  - A *senior's clause*, which can lower a tax rate, or exempt a portion of the assessed value from the tax calculation.

---

[30] "Are You Paying Too Much in Taxes?", NTU.org, https://bit.ly/3O0ywHC

- A *veteran's clause*, which may offer a property tax reduction for vets.
- A *disabled clause*, which may offer a property tax deduction for fully disabled people.

Hearty Serving

- Appeal the appraised value of property based on both errors and comparables. Get your assessment lowered and reduce your taxes.
- Savings: $100 monthly

Light Serving

- A 65-year-old widow files for a Homestead Exemption in her county, shielding $50,000 of property from taxation
- Savings: $50 monthly

Yield

Servings	Monthly Savings	10-Year × 173	20-Year × 521	30-Year × 1226
Hearty	$100	$17,300	$52,100	$122,600
Light	$50	$8,650	$26,050	$61,300
Your info				

Not bad. Don't waste any of those savings. Spoon them straight into your debts. Or, use them to add a monthly helping to your investments.

Glazed Gas Bill

$ $ 🍴🍴

Paying natural gas bills is a joyless experience. It's not as if you get something fun in return for sending them money. It's a bit like a roof repair, a speeding ticket, or losing a bet to your brother-in-law.

The average US gas bill is about $100 monthly. In larger or less-efficient homes (or more Northerly ones), heating bills can easily be double that. So, the savings are no small potatoes.

Ingredients

- Consider a home energy audit to find the highest-return projects. Check for utility, municipality, or state grants.
- Programmable thermostats can lower gas costs in the winter by 10%. The Wi-Fi ones even have apps that let you control your heating and cooling remotely. Cool! Or, in this case, warm.
- Better weather stripping can save 10%. Use a stick of lit incense or a piece of Christmas tinsel to find breezes around windows and doors. Seal around any pipes that lead outside.
- Improved attic insulation can save another 10-20%. Hire a reputable contractor or DIY by watching YouTube videos.
- Keeping furnace filters clean can save 5%.
- Consider switching from baths to showers.
- Replace your showerheads with low-flow models.
- Use the cold-water setting on your washing machine.
- Upgrade to high-efficiency windows at replacement time. Replace any windows that appear foggy.
- High-efficiency furnaces are generally worth the incremental costs—this can be assessed during your energy audit.

Hearty Serving

- Two properties, total gas bill of $317 monthly
- Install two programmable thermostats to save $32
- Air seal doors, windows, and gaps to save $32
- Improve attic insulation in both homes to save $48
- Replace furnace filters every 2 months to save $7 (net of filters)
- Savings: $119 monthly

Light Serving

- Small house, gas bill of $125 monthly
- Install a programmable thermostat to save $12
- Air seal doors, windows, and gaps to save $13
- Improve attic insulation to save $13
- Replace furnace filters every 2 months to save $4 (net of filters)
- Savings: $42 monthly

Yield

Servings	Monthly Savings	10-Year × 173	20-Year × 521	30-Year × 1226
Hearty	$119	$20,587	$61,999	$145,894
Light	$42	$7,266	$21,882	$51,492
Your info				

These savings amounts and percentages are approximate, given the country's various climates, home types and conditions. Temperatures vary, so examine your spending over a two- to three-year period. Some ideas may require out-of-pocket spending. Deduct that one-time cost from the total savings in the yield table.

Emulsified Electric Bill

$ $ ⚡⚡

The average US household spends about $115 a month for electricity. As with a gas bill, there's no joy in sending cash to the electric company. Let's whip up a juice reduction.

Ingredients

- Exorcise that phantom power. Plugged-in computers, stereos, and other gadgets can draw over $200 a year, even when they're off. Spooky. Get smart power bars or unplug what's not in use.

- Reduce air conditioner use. Try a programmable thermostat and settings that are slightly warmer than your norm. An air-conditioned house doesn't have to feel like a meat locker.

- Switch to LED lightbulbs that use 80% less energy. The light looks fine if you get "warm white" for most rooms and "daylight" for garages and laundry areas.

- If your utility uses time-of-use electric metering, run washers, dryers, and dishwashers during low-rate times when rates can be 50% lower. Set your dishwasher delay feature for this purpose.

- Clean the lint screen after every dryer load to dry faster and cheaper. The auto-dry function saves sprinting back and forth to the laundry to room to add another five or ten minutes.

- Consider a solar-powered clothes dryer, AKA a clothesline. Fresh-smelling clothes and a big reduction to your electric bill.

- Your mother was right: Putting on a sweater is way cheaper than using a space heater, which can use $60 a month or more.

- Lose the old beer fridge. It's cracking open at least $20 a month.

- Cover the pool to save 30-50% on heater costs.

- Simply turning things off when not in use is helpful but runs contrary to the approach of most teenagers. And some spouses.

Hearty Serving

- Two properties, total electricity bill of $333 monthly
- Reduce air conditioner use to save $17
- Remove rarely used second fridge to save $20
- Use swimming pool cover when not in use to save $67
- Replace 20 most-used lightbulbs with LEDs to save $20
- Time-shift appliance use to save $16
- Savings: $140 monthly

Light Serving

- Small house, electricity bill of $150 monthly
- Reduce air conditioner use to save $10 monthly
- Switch furnace fan to "auto" from "on" to save $18 monthly
- Replace ten most-used lightbulbs with LEDs to save $10
- Reduce use of portable electric heaters to save $12
- Time-shift appliance use to save $8 monthly
- Savings: $58 monthly

Yield

Servings	Monthly Savings	10-Year × 173	20-Year × 521	30-Year × 1226
Hearty	$140	$24,220	$72,940	$171,640
Light	$58	$10,034	$30,218	$71,108
Your info				

There are dozens of ways to take the brulé torch to your electricity bill with minimal investment and effort. Experiment and look at your annual power summary on your bill to check on your progress.

Marinated Mortgage Rate

$ $ 🍷 ♟ ♟ ♟

Even if your checking account, savings account, credit cards, and investments are all with one bank, don't feel compelled to get your mortgage there, too. Almost half of borrowers only consider one lender, and 77% only apply to a single lender.[31] This approach can leave a lot of money on the table.

Shopping for mortgages is a bit like selecting fruit. You shouldn't buy the first cantaloupe you see. You need to do a good deal of sniffing, squeezing, and tapping before selecting.

Ingredients

- Start by web shopping for rates at the major banks.
- Extend your search to smaller banks and credit unions.
- Look at online mortgage comparison sites.
- Connect with a licensed mortgage broker to see their options.
- In addition to the rate, be sure to compare:
  - Terms and conditions
  - Fees and penalties
  - Pre-approvals
  - Portability, renewal rates, and other features
  - Stability of the lender
- If you already have a mortgage and rates have fallen since you signed, approach your existing lender about refinancing to see if they can provide savings without an extensive application process.

---

[31] "Consumers' mortgage shopping experience", Consumer Financial Protection Bureau, January 2015, https://bit.ly/3ux2o72

Hearty Serving

- $500,000 mortgage at 5.2%; 30-year term, payments of $2,746
- Secure mortgage at 4.7% instead
- Difference in monthly payments of $153
- Difference in balance remaining at ten years: $6,157, at 20 years: $8,582

Light Serving

- $250,000 mortgage at 5.2%, 30-year term, payments of $1,373
- Secure mortgage at 4.7% instead
- Difference in monthly payments of $76
- Difference in balance remaining at ten years: $3,078 at 20 years: $4,291

Yield

Servings	Monthly Savings	10-Year × 173	20-Year × 521	30-Year × 1226
Hearty	$153	$32,626	$88,295	$187,578
Light	$76	$16,226	$43,887	$93,176
Your info				

*For the 10-, 20- and 30-year calculations, the number includes the future value of the payment difference, plus the remaining balance.

Fricasseed Furnishings

$ $ ¶¶

Ever try to sell home furnishings you no longer want? They're about as appealing to others as last month's leftovers, and just as challenging to sell. With luck, you might get ten cents on the dollar.

But turn that idea around the other way. Why not shop for some of your home furnishings and accessories from online marketplaces? The bigger and bulkier the item, the better the deal to be had. Check online listings and apps: I bet there are several pristine appliances, desks, and couches listed that need to be gone by Friday, if not sooner.

Ingredients
- For large items, use local sites like Craigslist, Freecycle, and OfferUp.
- For lighter pieces, extend your search to eBay.
- Most online marketplaces let you set up search alerts, which send an email when the item you want becomes available. Very cool. Bargain hunting, but without the hunting.
- Check out garage and estate sales. Let your friends know what you're looking to find.
- Be patient. If you're willing to wait a bit, you can likely get what you need for a fraction of the price of a new one.

What's out there? You name it! From carpets to couches, lighting to dining room sets, someone is selling it—even full sets of kitchen cabinets and beautiful artwork. For outdoors, there are high-end patio furniture, trampolines, and fire pits. Beautiful pianos are often free. Do some searching and get inspired!

| Be alert for bed bugs before bringing anything home. |

Hearty Serving
- One home and one vacation property
- Save $167 monthly on average on home furnishings
- Examples: dining room set, or a few pieces of art and a living room carpet in a year
- Savings: $167 monthly

Light Serving
- One home
- Save $83 monthly on average on home furnishings
- Examples: a set of bar stools and a coffee table, or a couch and some side chairs in a year
- Savings: $83 monthly

Yield

Servings	Monthly Savings	10-Year × 173	20-Year × 521	30-Year × 1226
Hearty	$167	$28,891	$87,007	$204,742
Light	$83	$14,359	$43,243	$101,758
Your info				

Instead of feeling desperate to get that new couch or coffee table this weekend, relax and enjoy the hunt for the perfect piece!

Roasted Repairs

$ $ $ ⍦⍦

Enough with expensive home repairs that pack a punch like a Szechuan hotpot. Before calling a pro, consider home fixing. With the help of YouTube videos, I fixed a clogged gas stove jet with a paperclip, a leaking fridge with a turkey baster (don't ask!) and replaced a broken ice maker with just a screwdriver. I nearly replaced a $1,000 gas dryer before diagnosing that it needed a new $12 door switch. Each repair took less than 30 minutes, using things I had around the house. Great savings, very satisfying, and proud stories you can use to bore your kids.

Ingredients

- Recruit a talented handy friend. Get the current job done and learn how to do it yourself for next time. Sometimes pros will work with you to save costs and let you learn.
- Search YouTube for any home fix-it job and let people with experience show you how it's done.
- For appliance repair, search on YouTube for repair videos.
- Search pro home fix-it websites for exact instructions.[32]
- Do an internet search for local building codes to ensure your work is being done safely.
- If you decide to contract the work, always get three estimates.

- Always wear appropriate safety gear.
- Don't attempt a repair that is beyond your capabilities.

---

[32] Check the Housing area of the Ingredients section of CashflowCookbook.com for specific repair sites.

Start with the mundane, such as learning how to clean gutters, change furnace filters, and replace door handles. Then, move up to such projects as installing light fixtures, unclogging drains, painting a room, or replacing a faucet. Still enjoying the DIY? Try installing ceramic tiling, fixing a washing machine, or installing shelving.

Hearty Serving

- One home and one vacation property
- Save the labor cost on $250 in projects on average monthly
- Examples: Replacing boards on a deck, replacing a refrigerator icemaker, or painting bedrooms
- Savings: $250 monthly

Light Serving

- One home
- Save the labor cost on $100 in projects on average monthly
- Examples: clearing drains a couple of times, installing shelving, and replacing a broken faucet
- Savings: $100 monthly

Yield

Servings	Monthly Savings	10-Year × 173	20-Year × 521	30-Year × 1226
Hearty	$250	$43,250	$130,250	$306,500
Light	$100	$17,300	$52,100	$122,600
Your info				

Great savings, plus the satisfaction of doing the work yourself.

Spatchcocked Self-Storage

$ $ $ 🍸 🍸

Ever get the sense that your home is bursting with excessive effluvia? Maybe it's the garage that has no room for your car, the basement you can't walk through, or the closets that rain objects down upon you as you open the door.

Perhaps you've slipped the surly bonds of your home and expanded your empire to include a storage locker that's squeezing your budget like a lemon.

Ingredients

Embark on a big purge of the junk you don't need, including:

- Anything you haven't touched in more than two years. This includes the boxes that contain you-know-not-what.

- Broken things? Get them fixed, sold, or discarded.

- Stuff you are storing for offspring who have grown and moved away: Send it to them. Postage due.

- Boxes of clothing you haven't worn in years. Ladies, that includes your 1980s power suits with the NFL shoulder pads. Gents, it's those oversized suits with the high waists and pleated pants. Donate or get them altered to a more modern state.

- Furniture that doesn't work in your current home. It's unlikely to work with your next home, either. Or the one after that!

- Documents, including copies of old electric bills, restaurant and grocery receipts, owner's manuals of things that you no longer own, benefit binders from former employers, and tax records older than the required holding period.

Organizing guru Marie Kondo talks about keeping only things that give you joy. Great concept. There is limited joy from your broken vacuum cleaner. Even less joy in your kid's old playpen, with dried barf on the rails. Especially now that she's retired.

Be ruthless. It's time for a yard sale, online listings, or a helpful donation. Some charities will even pick things up. Then add shelving or cabinets to free up space for those things you decide to keep.

Now it's time to eliminate or downsize your storage locker. Add up the value of what you're storing there. If you couldn't sell it all for $1,000, does it make sense to pay hundreds a month to store it?

Hearty Serving
- Large, climate-controlled storage locker at $450 monthly
- Eliminate need for locker entirely
- Savings: $450 monthly

Light Serving
- Medium-sized locker at $250 monthly
- Downsize to small locker for $150 monthly
- Savings: $100 monthly

Yield

Servings	Monthly Savings	10-Year × 173	20-Year × 521	30-Year × 1226
Hearty	$450	$77,850	$234,450	$551,700
Light	$100	$17,300	$52,100	$122,600
Your info				

Incredible. Over a half million dollars over 30 years to store stuff you will likely throw out when you retire—or that your heirs will relegate to a dumpster when you die.

Takeout Container - Housing

In this section, we looked at ten areas that can earn a potential $106,186 for our Light Serving and $280,535 for the Hearty Serving over ten years when invested at 7%:

✓ **Smart home protection.** Discount home alarm companies can be a low-calorie alternative.

✓ **Grab a shovel.** Consider splitting a snow blower, and snow clearing duty, with a neighbor.

✓ **Dare to compare.** Check for proper insurance coverage, combine home and car insurance, shop around for the best rate.

✓ **Adjust those property taxes.** Check the appeals process in your area.

✓ **Stop wasting heat.** Install programmable thermostats, clean furnace filters, improve weather stripping and attic insulation.

✓ **Find the electricity wasters.** Install LED lighting, remove extra refrigerators, and cut power to unused electronics.

✓ **Manage the mortgage.** Shop aggressively for the best mortgage and terms and renegotiate existing mortgages where possible.

✓ **Furnish savings.** Shop online for used furnishings.

✓ **Fix it yourself.** Sharpen your basic home repair skills with YouTube videos and books.

✓ **Empty the locker.** Estimate the value of what you're storing compared to the monthly storage cost. Get rid of stuff you don't need.

Continuously look at your recurring housing costs to find ways to improve. Check out the Ingredients section at CashFlowCookbook.com for products and services that may help.

Transportation

TRANSPORTATION COSTS CONSUME more than 14% of the average U.S. household budget.[33] It's enough to drive your finances into the ditch.

Next up is a set of recipes to grill those costs one by one. Car expenses are easy to miss—a half tank of gas here, a car wash there, and another $20 for parking. Not a big deal...until you add everything up. A brand-new, leased SUV can easily cost more than $1,200 per month, including payments, gas, maintenance, parking, and insurance. Even an economy car can still run over $300 per month.

Here are the basics for significant savings:

- Buy a gently used but well-maintained vehicle.
- Keep your vehicle for several years.
- Buy brands with a history of reliability.
- Follow the factory maintenance schedule.
- Get a vehicle that meets your needs 95% of the time.
- Learn eco-driving techniques and combine trips.
- Drive less by walking, biking, taking transit, carpooling.

Those are just the appetizers. Let's break out the Ginsu knives to do some major transportation cost-chopping.

---

[33] Karen Bennett, "What Americans spend: A look at the cost of housing, food, transportation and more," Bankrate.com, January 2022, https://bit.ly/3Ji36Jm

Tenderized Traffic

Cars are expensive, which is why we have a section devoted to them. One great way to save is by optimizing your route on every trip. There are lots of free smart phone navigation apps that optimize your route by knowing the speed limits, the speed of other drivers, and the info that others provide to the app, such as speed traps, accidents, and construction delays. Follow these apps for the best route and save a good 5% on reduced driving time, gas, mileage, wear and tear, and repairs. Delicious!

You can see this working when the app reroutes you onto an obscure side road after you see one-third of the drivers ahead take the same unmarked digital detour. The rest of the "suckahs" stay on the main road heading, unknowingly, straight into the jam.

As a bonus, you can end arguments with yourself or your partner as to which route is the best. Let the app optimize your routing. Find something new to argue about!

Ingredients

- Download a smartphone navigation app, or a similar real-time traffic app, to your smartphone.
- Let the app navigate; enjoy an optimized route on every trip.
- Check the app settings for options to save on tolls and fuel.
- Use the app to check for public transit or bike routes—maybe you don't need to drive.
- Save on gas, maintenance, arguments, and time.

Beet the traffic. Beet the costs. Beet wasted time. Sorry; couldn't resist.

- Use your car's onboard navigation, CarPlay, or Android Auto to connect to your phone.
- Older car? Get one of those nifty clamps for your phone that attaches to an air vent or coffee cup holder in your car. This saves you from holding it while you drive (illegal) or trying to catch it as it slides across your dashboard or falls under your seat (likely even worse).
- Activate the turn-by-turn voice instructions so you don't need to look at the screen.
- No peeking at your email, stock prices, or Facebook feeds with your phone perched up there! Stay focused on your driving.

Hearty Serving

- Two cars
- Total of $400 in gas + $300 in repairs = $700 of expenses
- Save 5% through reduced car use using optimized routing.
- Savings: $35 monthly

Light Serving

- One car
- $200 in gas + $50 in repairs = $250 of expenses
- Save 5% through reduced car use using optimized routing.
- Savings: $12 monthly

Yield

Servings	Monthly Savings	10-Year × 173	20-Year × 521	30-Year × 1226
Hearty	$35	$6,055	$18,235	$42,910
Light	$12	$2,076	$6,252	$14,712
Your info				

Trimmed Traffic Tickets

 $

Is it just me, or are there always police and parking enforcement people around at the wrong time? A three-minute jaunt to grab the dry cleaning: BAM! A trifle over the speed limit: POW!

Here's the math on parking tickets: Paid parking is always a fraction of the cost of a fine. If it means a bit of a walk, you get a free fitness bonus, too. It's almost always worth fighting traffic tickets. You'll often get a reduction in the fine or points for showing up and looking earnest.

Ingredients

- Slow down, savor the drive, keep your temper on simmer, and keep your money in your pocket.
- Leave the house ten minutes earlier to reduce stress and the need to speed.
- Take a minute to pay for street parking each trip.
- See if there's a parking app for your area that finds open spots, takes payment, and monitors meter time. Some of them even let you extend your parking time from your phone.
- Try fighting minor traffic tickets on your own to save the ticket and possible increased insurance premiums. If you win and the ticket is reduced, you'll save the ticket and possibly an insurance increase, too.
- For larger tickets, investigate a ticket fighting service.

> If you've been charged with impaired driving, dangerous driving, or other major infraction, get professional legal help.

Hearty Serving

- Two cars
- One parking ticket per car (2 × $25) = $50 monthly
- Use paid street parking for every trip = $10 monthly, saving $40 monthly
- One $120 traffic ticket per year, equivalent to $10 monthly, raising insurance by $8 monthly
- Fight ticket to lower it to $60, saving $5 monthly and saving insurance increase of $8
- Savings: $53 monthly

Light Serving

- One car
- One $25 parking ticket monthly
- Used paid street parking for every trip = $5 monthly
- Savings: $20 monthly

Yield

Servings	Monthly Savings	10-Year × 173	20-Year × 521	30-Year × 1226
Hearty	$53	$9,169	$27,613	$64,978
Light	$20	$3,460	$10,420	$24,520
Your info				

Nice savings and a lot less stress from worrying about getting and paying for parking tickets. With traffic tickets, simply drive carefully to avoid them.

Mashed Mall Trips

$ $ 🍸

Are shopping malls your idea of a good time? Nasty crowds, parking space battles, inflated prices, and a depressing food court.

And that's before the cost of driving. The cheapest way to drive your car is, well, not at all. We have come to think that buying something involves driving ourselves to the item and then driving ourselves and the item back home. A bit odd really. And inefficient.

Sometimes, we drive to the mall when we don't need anything and just look for things to buy. Even crazier.

Ingredients

- Consider whether you really need the item you're planning to get—don't shop just to shop.
- Can you walk or bike to a local store and skip the driving?
- Can you buy it online? Amazon is usually the price leader, but not always. Check pricing among Amazon, the online channel of your retailer, and warehouse clubs such as Costco, then look for used items on eBay, OfferUp or Craigslist.
- For clothing, try items on in the store for size, then next time save the trip and order from the same retailer online.
- Sign up for email updates from your favorite retailers. Savings can be significant—20, 30, even 40% isn't unusual. Set a rule, so the emails are routed to a shopping folder to keep the junk mail out of your inbox and reduce impulse buying.

This recipe is so versatile, it could have gone in multiple chapters: It saves on impulse buying, gas, parking tickets, car repairs, and your time. Before you go online or to the store for something, do a quick check that you actually need the item. Maybe borrowing or renting will do the trick. Check to see what might be lurking at the back of your closet.

Hearty Serving
- Two cars, weekly mall trips
- Total expenses of $400 gas + $300 repairs = $700 monthly
- Reduce car use, saving 10%
- Savings: $70 monthly

Light Serving
- One car, occasional mall trips
- Expenses of $200 gas + $50 repairs = $250 monthly
- Reduce car use, saving 5%
- Savings: $12 monthly

Yield

Servings	Monthly Savings	10-Year × 173	20-Year × 521	30-Year × 1226
Hearty	$70	$12,110	$36,470	$85,820
Light	$12	$2,076	$6,252	$14,712
Your info				

Apply your money savings to your debt or investments. By not sitting in traffic for an hour, you have time savings, too. Invest them in exercise, clean up your work emails, and make it to your kid's soccer game.

Creamed Car Loans

Financially, cars are a toxic soup of depreciation, interest expenses, maintenance, and gas bills. Few things are worse for your finances than something that *loses value* as you *pay interest* to own it. Minimizing any part of this hot mess is a great way to improve your monthly finances and reduce the negative impact on your wealth.

Car financing is a great place to start. The most common loan term is now six years (72 months),[34] and more than 85% of vehicles are financed.[35] Worse, only one in five buyers look at the total interest paid when shopping for a loan.[36] Let's get to work on those costs.

Ingredients

- Car loans start with the car, and the easiest way to save on depreciation and interest cost is to simply buy less car. Look at cheaper vehicles, demonstrators, used cars, or smaller models.

- If possible, buy a car at a time when dealers can't give them away. During the financial crisis of 2008-2009, dealerships were dead quiet. Prices were slashed and financing was as low as 0%. It happened again when COVID-19 hit in 2020.

- At the time of purchase, shop the financing. You're not committed to getting financing from your car dealer.

---

[34] Ronald Montoya, "How Long Should a Car Loan Be?" Edmunds.com, April 2022, https://edmu.in/37z2OAN
[35] I. Mitic, "Car Loan Statistics That Will Make You Want a Bicycle," fortunly.com, March 2022, https://bit.ly/3DW1P9Z
[36] "Study: how are Americans buying cars?' LexingtonLaw.com, April 2021, https://bit.ly/3NZDG71

- If you already have a car loan, try refinancing the loan with an online refinancing provider to save about $100/month.
- Keep your credit rating high. It has a big impact on overall interest cost. Check out the Crusted Credit Rating recipe.

> For massive savings, skip the vehicle entirely. Share or rent a car, carpool, use a bike, or your feet to get to work.

Hearty Serving
- Buy a demonstrator that is one model down from your preferred car, lowering the purchase price from $36,000 to $33,000.
- Shop the loan to lower the rate from 5.7% to 3.8%
- Savings: $86 in monthly payments

Light Serving
- Refinance an existing loan
- Loan is $25,000 at 5.7% with 5 years left. Refinance at 3.8%.
- Monthly savings: $22

Yield

Servings	Monthly Savings	10-Year × 173	20-Year × 521	30-Year × 1226
Hearty	$86	$14,878	$44,896	$105,436
Light	$22	$3,806	$11,462	$26,972
Your info				

The sharp chefs among you might ask how we can calculate ten-, twenty- and thirty-year wealth increases on a five-year car loan. Extra dessert for you! The calculations use these same principles on any future vehicles that you might buy. Note that we only used a couple of ingredients in this recipe—combine them for a tastier dish!

Carved Car Repairs

$ $ 🌱🌱🌱

Whoops. You just discovered some white scratches on your fender. You don't recall scraping anything and your spouse isn't fessing up. Your car dealer likely gave you a knowing smile and an estimate north of $1,500—enough to cancel some of your great savings work so far.

Or, perhaps your dealer has said it's time for your cabin air filter to be replaced for $85. Amazon likely has the part for about $25. But who knows how to replace filters? Only the dealer knows the magic recipes to repair scratched fenders and replace air filters.

Or, is there another way?

Ingredients

- Use the magic of YouTube to reveal repair secrets like these and many more:
  - A scratch repair kit (about $25) can buff out light scratches in a few minutes to save your fender and about $1,475.
  - You can replace your cabin air filter in about 5 minutes with no tools. Save about $50 in ten minutes. Ask the YouTube.
- Follow your manufacturer's schedule for maintenance, and don't buy into "seasonal specials" unless they align with the maintenance schedule.
- Shop around for expensive replacement parts like tires. Check two or three tire places, big-box stores, and your dealer online you may see price differences of 15% or more. This research might take 30 minutes, but it can save you $100–$200.

- If you're not comfortable doing a repair yourself, or if the process looks too complex, might void your warranty, or compromise safety, get it done at the dealer.
- If you're driving an Aston Martin, a Bentley, or a Lamborghini, don't be messing about. Get the car to the dealer. Or, better still, trade it in on something more economical.
- Check Yelp to see what others say about repair options.

Hearty Serving
- Two cars in the household
- Do it yourself on $100 of projects monthly
- Examples: replacing bulbs, batteries, engine air and cabin air filters, or price shopping for tires.
- Savings: $100 monthly

Light Serving
- One car in the household
- Do it yourself on $50 of projects monthly
- Examples: removing scratches with polishing compound; replacing bulbs, cabin and engine air filters, and wiper blades
- Savings: $50 monthly

Yield

Servings	Monthly Savings	10-Year × 173	20-Year × 521	30-Year × 1226
Hearty	$100	$17,300	$52,100	$122,600
Light	$50	$8,650	$26,050	$61,300
Your info				

The joy of new knowledge and freed-up cashflow. Get that cash working for you with a debt reduction or an investment infusion.

Deviled Driving Habits

$ $ ⚱

Fast acceleration. Hard braking. Lurching forward and back. Ever follow someone like that? Any chance you drive like that?

A few simple changes to your driving style can save you an incredible 35% on gas and repairs,[37] keep you out of court and offer your passengers (including the four-legged ones) a more comfortable ride.

Ingredients

- Accelerate gradually and smoothly.
- Look at traffic ahead and release the gas pedal if you see cars slowing. Coast for a bit before braking. Usually, traffic picks up and you save gas and maintenance. Don't hit anyone.
- Combine trips to save total mileage.
- Don't carry extra junk in your trunk, especially heavy stuff.
- Keep your tires inflated to the correct pressure. Check your car manufacturer's recommendation, usually found on a label on the driver-side door jamb.
- Don't idle the car for more than a minute. Modern engines don't need long warmups.
- Slow down on the highway. Doubling your speed quadruples the wind resistance and slices your fuel economy.

Do an internet search for eco-driving for more information. Cars use the least gas when driven at a constant, moderate speed. The less braking and accelerating, the better. Imagine an egg between

---

[37] Philip Reed, "We Test the Tips", Edmunds.com, April 2009, https://edmu.in/3v74TvI

your foot and the brake and another between your foot and the gas pedal. Easy does it. Of course, go ahead and scramble that egg if you need to avoid an accident.

You may be able to double the mileage between brake replacements, reduce tire wear, and make lots of other parts last longer. Like anything else, 30 days makes a habit. If your car has a fuel consumption display, check it every now and again to see the difference your new driving style makes.

Hearty Serving
- Two cars
- Total expenses of $400 gas + $300 repairs = $700 monthly
- Apply better driving techniques, saving 20%
- Savings: $140 monthly

Light Serving
- One car
- Expenses of $200 gas + $50 repairs = $250 monthly
- Apply better driving techniques, saving 20%
- Savings: $50 monthly

Yield

Servings	Monthly Savings	10-Year × 173	20-Year × 521	30-Year × 1226
Hearty	$140	$24,220	$72,940	$171,640
Light	$50	$8,650	$26,050	$61,300
Your info				

No investment required: just smoother, smarter, and safer cruising. Get those savings driving some wealth—use them to reduce debt or increase monthly savings contributions.

Caramelized Car Insurance

$ $ ⍦⍦

Most of the time, your car insurance just sits there quietly, like that bag of spinach rotting at the back of your fridge. All that changes if you get into an accident, after which the details of your policy become appetizing, like a steaming bowl of shiitake risotto. Having the right coverage is important, and it has never been easier to make sure that you're getting it at the right price.

Ingredients

- Adequate liability insurance on your vehicle policy is always a must, but older cars may be better suited to lower levels of comprehensive and collision insurance.
- Compare rates at different deductibles and pick the highest deductible you can afford.
- Shop around for rates and coverage. Try one of the online car insurance quoting tools, as well as a qualified independent broker.
- Bundle home and car insurance for 10–15% savings. If you have a vacation property, add that in for bigger savings.
- Consider accepting a driving monitoring device from the insurance company to save another $10-20 per month.
- Slow down, drive gently, and reduce premium-inflating tickets.
- Pay annually vs monthly for more savings.
- If you have college-aged kids away at school, call your insurance company and let them know. They will often lower the premium since the little darlings aren't using your car while they're away.

Hearty Serving

- Two cars (one newer), three drivers
- Total premium of $384 monthly
- Increase the deductibles from $500 to $1,000, saving $28 monthly
- Shop coverage like-for-like, saving $150 monthly
- New premium, $206 monthly
- Savings: $178 monthly

Light Serving

- One older car, one driver
- Total premium of $147 monthly
- Increase the deductible from $500 to $1,000, saving $14
- Bundle with home insurance, saving $19 monthly
- New premium, $114 monthly
- Savings: $33 monthly

Yield

Servings	Monthly Savings	10-Year × 173	20-Year × 521	30-Year × 1226
Hearty	$178	$30,794	$92,738	$218,228
Light	$33	$5,709	$17,193	$40,458
Your info				

Not bad for an hour's worth of work every few years! Get the freed-up cashflow marinating for you with debt reduction or increased investment contributions.

Crushed Commuting Costs

$ $ $ 🍴 🍴

In 2019, the average US commute was 28 minutes each way, and 86% of people drove to work.[38] For many, the daily commute is the biggest single use of their car. Often the car has only one occupant.

With a bit of organizing and planning, there are numerous ways to pare down commuting costs. COVID caused a paradigm shift as we learned about remote work. Let's now consider some alternatives to the commute—the savings are worth it.

Ingredients

- Can you work closer to where you live? Or vice versa? Does your employer have another location closer to your home? Can you work there some of the time? Can you continue working from home, at least part time?
- Set up a carpool—post a notice at work and online or try an online carpool app.
- Work from home one day a week—save 20% of your commuting costs and free up time. How about 2 or 3 days?
- With Uber, look at using the Pool and Express Pool option, sharing your ride to save 50% or more on UberX rates.
- Look at using public transit if you can. Compare the costs with driving. It might be worth doing this even a day or two a week.
- Ride your bike to work. See if your workplace has bike storage and showers. Bonus: Your commute and workout become one.

---

[38] Charlynn Burd et al, "Travel Time to Work in the United States: 2019 American Community Survey Reports," Census.gov, March 2021, https://bit.ly/3jkV08c

Which of these ideas can work for you? Challenge yourself to find a creative commuting recipe you like.

Hearty Serving

- One person commuting
- Spending $200 gas + $300 parking + $50 maintenance + $100 tolls
- Total commuting costs, $650 monthly
- Carpooled to save 50%
- New cost: $325 monthly
- Savings: $325 monthly

Light Serving

- One person commuting
- Spending $150 gas + $50 maintenance
- Total commuting costs, $200 monthly
- Worked from home 1 day a week to save 20%
- New cost: $160 monthly
- Savings: $40 monthly

Yield

Servings	Monthly Savings	10-Year × 173	20-Year × 521	30-Year × 1226
Hearty	$325	$56,225	$169,325	$398,450
Light	$40	$6,920	$20,840	$49,040
Your info				

Incredible savings. Well worth taking the time to find a lower-cost option. If you have two or more commuters in the family, rethink each of them. Can you boil things down enough to shift from two cars to one?

Sauteed SUV Savings

$ $ $ 🍴 🍴

Have you been biting off more car than you can economically chew?

OK, so you have kids. With lots of stuff. And friends. And a couple of dogs. And maybe it snows where you live and a big vehicle with all-wheel drive is helpful.

But how often do both parents have all the kids, the stuff, the friends, and the dogs in the car when it is snowing?

Rather than thinking of the cars as each belonging to one household driver, think of them as a fleet—a large and a small car, used by whomever has the need for the extra room that day.

Ingredients

- Keep one larger vehicle for moving the kids and gear, and a small commuter car for the spouse who is not on child duty.
- Consider a hybrid or electric vehicle for the commuter car. Much cheaper on fuel and maintenance. Government subsidies can also sweeten the pot.
- Have the little darlings walk, bike, or take public transit to school or their programs, if that is safe and workable where you live.
- Can one spouse bike or take transit to work and get rid of a car entirely?
- Could the "big" car be a minivan or a wagon instead of a gas-and-repair-hungry SUV?

- Buy gently used two or three-year-old cars instead of new ones—let someone else pay the depreciation while you get another six years+ of trouble-free driving.
- Keep your cars longer. Decent, well-maintained cars can easily last 200,000 miles.
- If you find yourself resisting change in this area, review the yield table below to whet your appetite for savings.

Hearty Serving
- Two SUVs
- Replace one SUV with an economy car
- Savings of $200 in gas, $50 in insurance, $50 in repairs and $200 is payments
- Savings: $500 monthly

Light Serving
- Two mid-sized cars
- Replace one mid-sized car with an economy car
- Savings of $100 in gas, $25 in insurance, $25 in repairs and $100 in payments
- Savings: $250 monthly

Yield

Servings	Monthly Savings	10-Year × 173	20-Year × 521	30-Year × 1226
Hearty	$500	$86,500	$260,500	$613,000
Light	$250	$43,250	$130,250	$306,500
Your info				

Big difference! Use *Consumer Reports* or the *Lemon-Aid Car Guide* to help find cars with great reliability and lower cost of ownership.

Poached Parking Expenses

$ $ $ ♟ ♟

If you pay to park for work each day, take time to consider cheaper alternatives.

Paying, say, $15 for a day of parking may not seem like a big deal. But at $15 for each of twenty-one working days a month, that's a monthly bill of $315, or $3,780 a year. At $30 per day, it adds up to $630 a month.

Ouch. Kind of like carrying the cake from the oven to the counter. Without oven mitts.

Ingredients

- Do an internet search for "find monthly parking" in your city.
- Use a parking app or website that displays available monthly parking spots with prices on a map around your workplace.[39] Awesome!
- Can you park for less near transit and use that for the last part of the commute?
- Does your building offer a discount for paying parking monthly rather than daily?
- Visit nearby condos and apartment buildings to see if they have extra spaces to rent.
- At the very least, do a stroll on a lunch hour and check the rates at other lots near your workplace.

---

[39] For the latest recommendations on parking apps and sites, see the Transportation section within the Ingredients tab on CashflowCookbook.com.

Hearty Serving

- Two cars commuting
- One car paying $30 daily for parking × 21 days = $630
- One car paying $20 daily for parking × 21 days = $420
- Total parking costs, $1,050
- Find two new parking spots at local condos for a total of $520
- Savings: $530 monthly

Light Serving

- One car commuting
- One car paying $20 daily for parking × 21 days = $420
- Find a new parking spot at local condo for $220
- Savings: $200 monthly

Yield

Servings	Monthly Savings	10-Year × 173	20-Year × 521	30-Year × 1226
Hearty	$530	$91,690	$276,130	$649,780
Light	$200	$34,600	$104,200	$245,200
Your info				

Wow. Making this change might take an hour of research and a five- or ten-minute walk to your new parking spot each day. You may need to season the math slightly if you drive to work only some days of the month. Be sure to do the research for each car commuting.

Serve with a freshly increased monthly car or mortgage payment or savor the rising balance in your investment account.

Takeout Container - Transportation

Cars are cool and convenient, but they take a huge bite out of your income. Try adding up the total cost of running your car for a year.

This section's ten recipes can save a potential total of $119,197 for our Light Servings and $348,941 for the Hearty Servings over ten years when invested at 7%:

✓ **Use the app.** Use navigation apps to cut commuting time by routing around traffic jams.

✓ **Tackle your tickets.** Drive responsibly and pay up front for parking. Fighting traffic tickets is worth the time. Avoiding them is better.

✓ **Stay home and click.** Do your shopping from home to purée fuel and parking costs, hassle, and time.

✓ **Pare the fat from your car loan.** Use some simple steps to reduce this interest cost.

✓ **Reduce the repairs.** Shop around for the best repair cost and learn some basic maintenance you can do yourself.

✓ **Drive gently.** Learn eco-driving techniques to crush fuel and repair costs.

✓ **Shop your insurance.** Look for the right insurance for your situation, combine with your home insurance, see if annual billing is cheaper, notify them when kids move out.

✓ **Creative commuting.** Bike, walk, carpool, take transit, and/or work from home.

✓ **Downsize.** What vehicles do you really need?

✓ **Park for less.** Look at alternative parking options.

Continuously look at your recurring transportation costs to find ways to improve. Check out the Transportation ideas in the Ingredients section at CashflowCookbook.com for services that can help.

Food & Drink

FOOD COSTS CONSUME ABOUT 10% of the average US budget,[40] so it's worth taking a bite out of them. Your health is even more important than your wealth and many of these recipes are beneficial to both. Certainly, they'll give you something to chew on.

Changes in these areas can make a difference:

- Choices: Save with generic food
- Meat: Consider the plant payoff
- Sale items: Load up when you can
- Lists: Buy what you need
- Frozen: Cheaper and less spoilage
- Loyalty cards: The easy way to save
- Snacks: Prepare and save
- Food waste: Big savings, easy habits
- Lunch prep: Healthy with a side of super savings
- Drinks: Minor habit or major cash drain?

But let's not take the fun out as we reduce the costs. A few simple changes can make a big difference with minimal sacrifice.

---

[40] Karen Bennett, "What Americans spend: A look at the cost of housing, food, transportation and more," Bankrate.com, January 2022, https://bit.ly/3Ji36Jm

Gingered Generics

 $

Years of brand advertising have sharpened our Pavlovian reflexes so that we think of brand names almost before we think of the actual product we need to buy. But right there, in those plain cans and boxes, may be easy savings. The beauty is more than label deep.

The cost of generic products averages about 25% less than nationally advertised brands. And many of them are made by the same companies. So why not splurge $1.69 on a tube of toothpaste or $2.69 on a jar of spaghetti sauce and find out? Worst case, you are out a couple of bucks. Best case, you have a new favorite and 25% savings on that part of your grocery bill. Forever.

Ingredients

- Try the generic products in each category—from canned and frozen foods to household needs like toilet paper, paper towels, cleaning products, and garbage bags.

- Get a *Consumer Reports* online subscription and check their reviews of generics to save your own testing.

- Check pricing when you shop. Sometimes the national brands are on sale, making them cheaper than the generics. There's no reason to go generic if old faithful is on sale.

- Make a shared list on your smartphone so you know which generic products made the grade. And share the list with any family members who help with the shopping.

Hearty Serving

- Family of five
- Grocery bill of $1,500 monthly
- Switch $400 worth to generics, saving 25%
- New bill of $1,400 monthly
- Savings: $100 monthly

Light Serving

- Single person
- Grocery bill of $400 monthly
- Switched $100 worth to generics, saving 25%
- New bill of $375 monthly
- Savings: $25 monthly

Yield

Servings	Monthly Savings	10-Year × 173	20-Year × 521	30-Year × 1226
Hearty	$100	$17,300	$52,100	$122,600
Light	$25	$4,325	$13,025	$30,650
Your info				

Not bad for easy brand substitutions. Keep experimenting to find generics you like. Lock in the benefit by accelerating debt repayment or increasing savings rate with the freed up cashflow.

Marinated Meat Reduction

$ $ Ⴤ

Meat makes up 22% of a typical grocery bill.[41] Moving to a vegan diet can reduce food costs by up to 34%.[42] Going all the way to vegetarian or vegan meals is a personal choice, but reducing meat by, even say, 30% may be helpful for both wallet and arteries. Is it time to put a steak in the ground? Or at least back in the display case?

Whether it's to help animals, save the planet, improve your health, or save money, reducing the carnivorous component of your groceries is worth a try. Think of fruits and vegetables as the mainstay and meat as an accompaniment.

Ingredients
- Move to smaller meat portions at each meal—3 oz may be enough.
- Have a couple of vegetarian or vegan days each week.
- Start exploring vegan or vegetarian recipes.
- Try vegetarian or vegan restaurants to get inspiration for your own cooking.

Like anything else, thirty days makes a habit. We tend to crave the foods we eat most. Focus on meat dishes and your shopping cart will steer itself in that direction. Eat more fruits and vegetables and your food fantasies will switch to big salads.

---

[41] Lam Thuy Vo, "What American Spends on Groceries," NPR Planet Money, June 8, 2012, npr.org, https://n.pr/3e7Fs8z

[42] Springmann et al., "The Global and Regional Costs of Healthy and Sustainable Dietary Patterns," thelancet.com, https://bit.ly/3QyCAjn

Hearty Serving

- Family of five
- Grocery bill of $1,500 monthly, including $300 of meat
- Switch $150 of meat to $50 of veggies and grains
- New bill: $1,400 monthly
- Savings: $100 monthly

Light Serving

- Single person
- Grocery bill of $400 monthly, including $100 of meat
- Switch $50 of meat to $20 of veggies and grains
- New bill: $370 monthly
- Savings: $30 monthly

Yield

Servings	Monthly Savings	10-Year × 173	20-Year × 521	30-Year × 1226
Hearty	$100	$17,300	$52,100	$122,600
Light	$30	$5,190	$15,630	$36,780
Your info				

Improve your net worth, spruce up your cardiovascular system and reduce global warming. Almost too good to be true.

Smoked Sale Bin

$ $ 🍸🍸🍽

On most shopping trips, you can score a few items on sale, such as cans of black beans for 30% off, or maybe your favorite toothpaste has shed a buck from its usual price. Not bad, but no one ever got rich on occasional savings on beans and toothpaste.

What you really need are those kinds of discounts on most of your groceries, forever. Why not actually make that happen?

Grocery stores run on thin margins, meaning they can't afford to offer large discounts all the time on all the stuff you need. So, they sprinkle them around to entice you in the door on the sale items, and then make their money on the rest.

But what happens when we turn that around? Let's focus our buying on the sale items, switching brands or even products to get to those 30–50% discounts. If the sale items are ones that keep, why not stock up with a few weeks' supply? Paper towels, frozen vegetables, garbage bags, canned goods, and coffee are all good candidates to buy when the price drops. It's also great to load up on these kinds of bulk non-perishables at warehouse clubs.

Experiment with your perishable consumption trends to ensure that you and your family can take down the large format containers. A gallon jug of ketchup, for example, is a deal only if you use it before it turns into a vat of nasty brown gunk.

Ingredients
- Stock up when non-perishable items go on sale.

- Substitute similar sale products. If you're seeking frozen blueberries and frozen raspberries are on sale, be bold and switch!
- Keep a smartphone list of well-stocked items or a pantry picture so as not to over-buy anything.

Pick up the grocery store's weekly flyer on your way into the store and adjust your list and meal plans around sale items.

Hearty Serving
- Family of five
- Grocery bill of $1,500 monthly
- Switch to buying $300 worth at 33% off
- New bill: $1,400 monthly
- Savings: $100 monthly

Light Serving
- Single person
- Grocery bill of $400 monthly
- Switch to buying $100 worth at 33% off
- New bill: $367 monthly
- Savings: $33 monthly

Yield

Servings	Monthly Savings	10-Year × 173	20-Year × 521	30-Year × 1226
Hearty	$100	$17,300	$52,100	$122,600
Light	$33	$5,709	$17,193	$40,458
Your info				

These are slow-cooker savings, but as you can see, they still add up over time.

Grilled Grocery List

$ $ $ 🍴 🍴

Stop me if you've heard this one: Your cart is almost full, you're cutting it close to get out of the store in time to drive someone to a piano lesson and BAM! Are those cookies half price? Should I just grab that block of cheese in case the kids get hungry after school? Hello! Check out that candy display!

We all know how this ends. The cookies are gone ten minutes after the kids find them, and that block of cheese takes the place of the moldy one you bought two weeks ago. You're not alone. In fact, 78% of us buy more than we intended when grocery shopping.

The easy lesson is to shop with a list. Less waste, fewer unneeded items, and food that fits a healthy meal plan. Group the list by food areas in the store to save zipping from one end of the store to the other. It's one thing to buy milk, yogurt, and cheese and then head to strawberries, blueberries, and bananas. It takes twice as long to shop for milk, strawberries, yogurt, blueberries, cheese, and then bananas.

Using a shopping list is an easy way to knock 10% off your grocery bill. You'll use the ingredients you already have, avoid buying stuff you don't need, and help prevent impulse buying. For the math below, we'll go with a conservative 7% savings.

Ingredients

- Take a moment to create a shopping list or try some of the shopping list apps from the App Store or Google Play, including ones from the grocery stores themselves.

- Spend time planning your meals for the week, so you know what ingredients you'll need.
- Before you head to the store, take a good look at what's in the fridge and the cupboards.
- Buy only what you need for that week's meals.
- Don't shop on an empty stomach.
- Keep the grocery list stuck to the fridge or in a shared smartphone list and train your family to add items they use up.

Hearty Serving
- Family of five
- Grocery bill of $1,500 month
- Use a list and don't shop when hungry to save 7%
- New grocery cost: $1,395 monthly
- Savings: $105 monthly

Light Serving
- Single professional
- Grocery bill of $400 monthly
- Use a list and don't shop when hungry to save 7%
- New grocery cost: $232 monthly
- Savings: $28 monthly

Yield

Servings	Monthly Savings	10-Year × 173	20-Year × 521	30-Year × 1226
Hearty	$105	$18,165	$54,705	$128,730
Light	$28	$4,844	$14,588	$34,328
Your info				

Buy only what you need for less food waste, less grocery store drama, and better health—and an earlier retirement.

Garnished Grocery Card

$ $ 🍸

To save on food, you could grow your own vegetables, drive to three grocery stores to chase bargains, and watch YouTube videos to learn about extreme couponing. Those of us with full time jobs, however, may want an easier approach to savings.

Cashflow Cookbook is all about freeing up cashflow with minimal effort and minimal sacrifice. For that, few investments beat the humble loyalty card from your main grocery store. The complex point systems seem to be designed by NASA retirees, but the bottom line is easy to understand. Signing up takes about ten minutes. At our local store, the 12-month rolling savings are printed on the bottom of the receipt. We clocked in $1,250 for just the two of us. Nothing to do but scan the card at checkout.

Ingredients

- Head to the customer service desk at your main grocery store or visit their website.
- Sign up for their loyalty card or app and keep it handy.
- Scan the card each time you buy groceries.
- Some grocery stores also have a branded credit card that gives a percent back on groceries. Do the math on that as well.
- Some loyalty programs offer occasional discounts on gift cards from other retailers. If the gift cards go on sale from one of your regular retailers, this is an opportunity for additional savings.
- The store may have featured items with additional savings. Check their flyer on online specials.

Hearty Serving

- Family of five
- Spending $1,500 on groceries each month
- Sign up for loyalty card, saving $150 monthly
- Total savings: $150 monthly

Light Serving

- Single person
- Spending $500 on groceries monthly
- Signs up for loyalty card, saving $50 monthly
- Savings: $50 monthly

Yield

Servings	Monthly Savings	10-Year × 173	20-Year × 521	30-Year × 1226
Hearty	$150	$25,950	$78,150	$183,900
Light	$50	$8,650	$26,050	$61,300
Your info				

OK, that was easy! Compare the grocery store programs and credit cards in your area to work your best deal. A bit of research, then a quick swipe on each visit. Easy money.

Fluted Frozen Food

$$ \raisebox{0pt}{\$}\raisebox{0pt}{\$}\,\Y$$

What if there was a way to get all kinds of food at a great discount—food that takes up no room in your fridge, stay fresh for months, and the leftovers store beautifully? And what if you could get fish, meat, fruit, vegetables, entrees, and appetizers with this technique?

Well, this magic exists, and it's known as frozen food. Making in-store comparisons, you will see that frozen food can range from 50% (berries) to 60% (vegetables) to 75% cheaper (fish filets). And that's just savings on the purchase price. The freshness and convenience add another whole set of benefits.

For years, I've made protein shakes that included spinach as an ingredient. I would buy a small package of fresh spinach each week, use a few leaves in each shake, then toss the leftover pungent green sludge at the end of the week. Eventually, I switched to frozen spinach at $1/7^{th}$ the cost with no waste. No one is getting rich on spinach savings, but you get the concept!

Ingredients

- Experiment with buying more frozen fruit, vegetables, and meat.
- Buy in quantity for better prices (especially at big box stores), then divide into smaller packages when storing in the freezer.
- Stock up when frozen goods are on sale.
- Freeze any food products that you can't eat in time.
- Defrost only what you need. Keep the rest carefully wrapped and frozen to reduce waste.

- Set up a recurring frozen food meeting with your grocery store every March--it's Frozen Food Month. Even bigger sales.

Hearty Serving

- Family of five
- Grocery bill of $1,500 monthly
- Meat, fruit, vegetables, and juice are 40% of the bill, or $600
- Switch 2/3 to frozen to save 40% ($160)
- New grocery cost: $1,340 monthly
- Savings: $160 monthly

Light Serving

- Single professional
- Grocery bill of $400 monthly
- Meat, fruit, and vegetables are 40% of the bill, or $160
- Switched 2/3 to frozen to save 40% or $43
- New grocery cost: $357 monthly
- Savings: $43 monthly

Yield

Servings	Monthly Savings	10-Year × 173	20-Year × 521	30-Year × 1226
Hearty	$160	$27,680	$83,360	$196,160
Light	$43	$7,439	$22,403	$52,718
Your info				

Making just this one change will save enough to match the total average American wealth at retirement. All from just making a switch to more frozen food. Yum.

Salted Snacks

$ $ ¥

The Snack Monster takes many forms. It could be vending machine snacks, a daily muffin with your coffee, late afternoon snack, or something for the commute home. Take a moment to tally your monthly spend and see if snack re-assessment is warranted.

The cost of machine snacks is at least triple the cost of buying the same snacks in bulk at a warehouse club or bulk food store, and online ordering may be cheaper still. Bring a case to the office and keep it under your desk. You can even cater meetings and increase your popularity. Coffee shop snacks are also far pricier than homemade fare. Can you bring something from home? And the priciest snacks are served in a hotel room mini bar. Stay out of there! Pack your own licorice, chocolate bars, and night caps.

Ingredients

- Instead of using a vending machine, buy snacks in bulk at warehouse clubs or big-box stores such as Costco, Sam's Club, or Walmart.
- Buy larger containers of snacks at your grocery store.
- Bring homemade snacks with you to the office.
- Increase work-from-home time to reduce all kinds of store-bought snacks.
- Use the savings to invest in high quality stocks. Check with your advisor about soda and potato chip companies.

Hearty Serving

- Two heavy snackers in the family
- Each one buys two $2 snacks per day for a total spending, $240 per month
- One quits the snacks, the other starts buying in bulk for half the cost
- New cost: 2 × $1 daily, or $60 monthly
- Savings: $180 monthly

Light Serving

- One light snacker in the family
- Buying one $2 snack per day for a total of $60 monthly
- Switched to buying snacks in bulk at half the cost
- New cost: $30 monthly
- Savings: $30 monthly

Yield

Servings	Monthly Savings	10-Year × 173	20-Year × 521	30-Year × 1226
Hearty	$180	$31,140	$93,780	$220,680
Light	$30	$5,190	$15,630	$36,780
Your info				

More than a dollop of savings. As always, make the change and commit the savings right away to debt reduction or increased savings. Imagine the family in the example above increasing their mortgage payment by $180 monthly and saving years of payments. Or investing their snack-based savings and covering a child's entire university education. A tasty proposition.

Frizzled Food Waste

$ $ $ ⍾⍾

Ever spend a nice day cleaning out your fridge? Didn't think so.

Ahh, the joy of rooting through packages of decomposing matter, questioning the expiration dates, or wondering why you even bought it in the first place. Sure makes you appreciate why you procrastinated on this project!

Spending a pile on groceries, then discarding them as toxic sludge just a few days later is no one's idea of a good time. Incredibly, we waste about 1/3 of the groceries we buy, or nearly $1,900 per year per household.[43] If ever there was a painless way to save money, it would be spending less on rotting food. I thought you might agree! Fire up the stove and let's frizzle away food waste.

Ingredients

- Plan your meals to minimize waste.
- Buy in quantities you can consume before expiration.
- Use one of the sites that suggest recipes based on what you have. Half an onion, a block of cheddar, mint leaves, and a can of pie filling could make...well...it works for other leftovers!
- Check in on your little fridge dwellers every couple of days and serve up anything getting a bit "post peak."
- Buy a set of fridge storage containers and save leftovers.
- Freeze anything that is surplus to current needs.

---

[43] Lana Bandoim, "The Shocking Amount of Food U.S. Households Waste Every Year," Forbes.com, Jan 2020, https://bit.ly/37c7CvS

Hearty Serving

- Family of five
- Grocery bill of $1,500 monthly
- Lower food waste from $500 to $200
- Savings: $300 monthly

Light Serving

- Single person
- Grocery bill of $400 monthly
- Lower food waste from $120 to $25
- Savings: $52 monthly

Yield

Servings	Monthly Savings	10-Year × 173	20-Year × 521	30-Year × 1226
Hearty	$300	$51,900	$156,300	$367,800
Light	$52	$8,996	$27,092	$63,752
Your info				

Better for the planet, less garbage to lug out, and enough money to buy a beautiful yacht for your retirement—just like the ones on the cover of your wealth or life insurance document folder.

Prepared Packed Lunch

$$\textrm{\$ \$ \$}$$

OK, it's hard to look like a big shooter when you take your lunch to the office. But look again. Once you do the math, you might decide that taking your lunch is the quickest way to become a big shooter.

And don't forget the health benefits. When you make your own lunch, you are less likely to eat something loaded with crap, because, well, you made it.

Yes, this one takes a bit of work. But it's easier than you think.

Ingredients

- The night before, make a big container of salad with your favorite protein on it—a bit of chicken, beans, or tofu. Pack a touch of dressing on the side to mix in at lunchtime. Or make a rice, bean, and frozen mixed vegetable combo, ready to microwave. Mix in different sauces for variety—black bean, pasta sauce, red curry, or chili powder with lime. Don't forget the after-lunch mints on some of these.

- Try making soup, lasagna, or chili, packaging it into lunch portions and taking that to work through the week. Or make two different dishes so you can alternate.

- Old school it with tasty sandwiches.

- Incorporate leftovers to reduce food waste.

- Invest in the right hardware. Look for salad containers with separate holders for dressings and stackable, microwaveable containers that provide all-in-one storage for several types of victuals.

- Buy a re-useable, insulated lunch bag to carry it all in, something dark and execu-looking.

Is all this worth it? Let's look.

Hearty Serving

- Couple eating work lunches out every day with a total of 16 restaurant lunches and 26 takeout lunches monthly
- Restaurant lunch bill of 16 × $25 = $400, plus takeout lunches of 26 × $14 = $364 for a total cost of $764 monthly
- Switch to half packed lunches: 8 restaurant lunches x $25 = $200, 13 takeout lunches x $14 = $42 and 21 packed lunches x $3 = $305
- Savings, $459 monthly

Light Serving

- Single professional
- 21 takeout lunches monthly at $14 each = $294
- New lunch cost, 21 × $3 packed lunches = $63
- Savings, $231 monthly

Yield

Servings	Monthly Savings	10-Year × 173	20-Year × 521	30-Year × 1226
Hearty	$459	$79,407	$239,139	$562,734
Light	$231	$39,963	$120,351	$283,206
Your info				

Looks like the brown bag routine is more appetizing than you thought! It's worth prep time Sunday nights to add more than a quarter of a million dollars to your retirement fund, don't you think? Or clear out a mortgage several years earlier? Maybe go ahead and dust off that Star Wars lunch box after all. Who's laughing now?

Drizzled Drinks

$ $ $ 🍸 🍸

Few expenditures get more financially flogged than the lowly latte. Surely a java jolt won't tip us into financial ruin. And if the whole idea was minimal effort and minimal sacrifice, is there not a way to spare the morning cup of joe?

Maybe. Start by assessing your actual monthly spend on paid drinks including soda, juice, and coffee and then you decide. If it is material, it might be worth changing a habit or two. Thirty days of water in place of soda, or home brewed coffee instead of store bought might change your habits and accelerate your early retirement plans.

Ingredients

- Add up your monthly spend on paid drinks and see whether a change is worth it.
- Every workplace has fresh, clean water available for free. Get a nice water bottle and keep cool water on hand to replace multiple soft drinks, bottled juices, and expensive coffees.
- If your addiction is too powerful, try drinking the coffee provided where you work instead of heading to the coffee shop. I know, you think it's horrible swill. But try a blindfolded taste test. If the java really is bad, lobby management for upgraded brew.
- Try brewing coffee or tea at home and taking it along in a travel mug. You can't complain about the coffee you made yourself!

Hearty Serving

- Family with two coffee and soda devotees
- Each buying two $5 coffees and one $2 soda per day, including weekends
- Total of $24 daily or about $720 monthly
- Switched to drinking company-provided coffee or water at work and using a personal water bottle on the weekend for $0 monthly
- Savings: $720 monthly

Light Serving

- One high-end coffee buyer
- Buying one $5 coffee per day, including weekends, for a total of $150 monthly
- Switched to drinking company coffee at $0 daily on workdays and home brewing Saturday and Sunday at $0.50 daily, for a total cost of $4 monthly
- Savings: $146 monthly

Yield

Servings	Monthly Savings	10-Year × 173	20-Year × 521	30-Year × 1226
Hearty	$720	$124,560	$375,120	$882,720
Light	$146	$25,258	$76,066	$178,896
Your info				

Yes, I did the math right. Adding nearly $900,000 to a retirement account is massive and the over-caffeinated family above could do that by changing their daily drinks! If your numbers are different, do your own math and add it to the bottom row of the Yield table. Bottoms up!

Takeout Container – Food & Drink

Food and drink are a big part of our lives, so there's no reason to carve them down to the bone. But we've learned that a few tweaks can make a big difference in our spending, without leaving a sour taste or taking away the fun.

In this section, we looked at ten ways to save up to $90,306 for our Light Serving and $410,702 for the Hearty Serving over ten years when invested at 7%:

✓ **Go generic.** Step away from the big brands. There's a whole generic world out there, which is typically 25% cheaper.

✓ **Eat less meat.** Reduce meat consumption for improved health and significant savings.

✓ **Love the sale bin.** Learn to stock up on sale items, particularly non-perishables, to save 25% or more.

✓ **Make a grocery list.** Take a list to the store and avoid purchasing things you already have or don't need.

✓ **Give yourself some chills.** Consider frozen fruits and vegetables. Less cost, less spoilage and easier to store.

✓ **Get a grocery loyalty card.** No cost, ten minutes. Real savings.

✓ **Reinvent snacks.** Switch to bulk snacks rather than single-serving ones.

✓ **Pack your lunch.** Some prep time on weekends can set you up with a week's worth of high nutrition at low cost.

✓ **Ditch the drinks.** All that high-end coffee and soda adds up. Make coffee at home or enjoy fresh, clean tap water.

Many of these ideas can become habits with a bit of practice.

Cashflow Cookbook

Household

OK, SO YOU'VE TRIMMED THE FAT from your housing, transportation, and food spending. Nice! That freed cash to pay down debt or increase your savings rate. Great progress. But let's get back to the kitchen. There are lots of new recipes to try out!

Savings on household expenditures may seem harder to track down than fresh loquat. Google it… I'll wait. But simple changes can make a big difference. Use these next ten recipes to reduce common household costs and apply the savings to wealth building.

Here are the areas we'll look at:

- Kids activities
- Cell phone bills
- Clothing
- Purchase timing
- Health care
- Comparison Shopping
- Learning
- Prescriptions
- Day care
- College

Stewed Sports Spending

Team sports and other activities provide kids with great exercise and a chance to learn about teamwork. But even with all the benefits, kids' programs can leave the family budget a little overcooked.

Let's look at ways of saving that can work whether your kids are into gymnastics, ski racing, football, or dance. Here are ideas on how to simmer down the cost of the main expenses.

Ingredients

- Buy used equipment to save 40% or more. Remember to check for safety certification, damage, overuse, and expiration dates. Check used sporting goods stores and local online marketplaces.
- Use early signups to save 10% on tournament and team fees. Consider becoming a team manager or coach for additional savings.
- Carpool to save 50% or more on transportation.
- Buy snacks in bulk. Make meals to pack for road trips to save 30%.
- At tournament time, use travel points, discount hotel sites, or Airbnb to save 10% or more.

Consider the overall cost of a sport before signing up for the first time—it's challenging to pull back on a sport once committed. Less gear-intensive sports like soccer can be less expensive. Also make sure that your child is fully invested before you invest.

Hearty Serving

- Family with three participants in sports or other paid activities
- Total monthly costs equivalent to $125 for equipment, $200 for fees, and $50 for driving expenses: total of $375
- Buy used and/or traded equipment to save $50
- Carpool to save another $25 monthly
- Register early to reduce fees by $25
- New total cost: $275
- Savings: $100 monthly

Light Serving

- Family with one participant in sports or other paid activities
- Monthly cost equivalent of $42 for equipment and $66 for fees = $108 monthly
- Buy used equipment or trade up to save $17
- Register early to reduce fees by $8
- New cost: $83 monthly
- Savings: $25 monthly

Yield

Servings	Monthly Savings	10-Year × 173	20-Year × 521	30-Year × 1226
Hearty	$100	$17,300	$52,100	$122,600
Light	$25	$4,325	$13,025	$30,650
Your Info				

*Assumes ten years of sports per child. Note that the 20 and 30-year value comes from continuing to grow the 10-year value at 7% for another ten years or twenty years.

Seared Cell Service

$ $ 🍴

For most families, the cost of mobile phone service is significant. Of course, the original business case for the kids' cell phones was about being able to stay in touch with them when they're out. Although they never miss a Snapchat or an Instagram update from their friends, some of these devices seem to misfire with incoming messages from the parents. Darn technology!

Cell phone costs are often overlooked as an area for savings. In most households, there's an ongoing tug-of-war to keep the bills reasonable, the data usage under control, and the phone out of the lake, the toilet, or the washing machine.

While you're not going to stop the gaming and YouTube consumption entirely, you can mince megabytes to serve up a manageable mobile bill each month.

Ingredients

- Check the data stats from your provider: What is the total monthly data consumption? Who is overusing and why?
- Use an online cell cost comparison tool to find the best deal.
- See if your company has a program that extends corporate pricing to employees. Such deals may also be offered by professional, and alumni associations.
- Get everyone on a family plan with one carrier.
- Ensure all the phones are set to use your home wi-fi rather than cellular; the same goes for other common locations like schools, offices, airports, and gyms.
- Get roaming packages when you travel.

- Call your provider each year to optimize your plan as your needs change—a one-hour call will yield significant savings. Make sure your provider knows that breaking up isn't so hard to do.
- Use apps like, Zoom, WhatsApp, or Facebook for free wi-fi calling to save on minutes, long distance, and roaming charges.

Hearty Serving
- Family with four cell phones
- Spending $300 monthly
- Comparison shop multiple carriers, optimize plans
- Set all phones to use wi-fi at frequent locations
- Monitor usage with an app
- New spending: $150 monthly
- Savings: $150 monthly

Light Serving
- Single person, one cell phone
- Spending $75 monthly
- Monitor usage with an app
- Call provider to optimize cost
- New spending: $45 monthly
- Savings: $30 monthly

Yield

Servings	Monthly Savings	10-Year × 173	20-Year × 521	30-Year × 1226
Hearty	$150	$25,950	$78,150	$193,900
Light	$30	$5,190	$15,630	$36,780
Your Info				

Season your long-term savings with the newfound cash and serve when you retire.

Caramelized Clothing Costs

$ $ 🍸 🍸

It's so fun to find a clothing bargain. Sure, it's a bit too big/small/boxy, but it's still a pretty good fit. And the color isn't my favorite, but how often do you find *that* label at 40% off?

Six months go by and there's that garment: forgotten at the back of your closet. Did you wear it to that important presentation? Nope. For your performance review? First date from Match? No, no, and "Are you kidding?" Each time we open our closet, we are looking for the best possible item. The fact is we only ever wear 20% of the clothing we buy. We sell the other 80%--often ten years later at a yard sale for five cents on the dollar. Or we just give it away. So, the biggest change to make in this area is to buy *only* when you really need something, and then, only when it is *perfect* in every respect.

Let's look at this in more detail. Americans spend about 3.8% of their income on clothing. An average reader of this book might spend $6,000 or more annually on clothing. Twenty percent of these items are worn and 80% ($4,800 worth), hang forgotten in the closest, are sold at a yard sale for next-to-nothing or given to charity. *That's burning nearly $5000 a year.*

If you bought only the best 20%—clothes that you'll actually wear—you could apply an extra $400 monthly for debt reduction or investment. You'd look just as great, free up all that shopping time and have a closet full of great clothes. Like walking up to a smorgasbord of just your favorite foods. Let's drain our old thinking about buying clothing and start fresh.

Ingredients

- Buy specific items that you need to fill a wardrobe gap.
- Get high-quality clothes with classic styling that fit perfectly.
- Only buy items that really excite you.
- Don't shop for the sake of shopping.
- For kids, buy practical or gently used, not designer items.
- Shop with a friend who will talk you out of impulse purchases.
- Keep receipts until you're sure, then return what you won't wear.

Hearty Serving

- Family with two adults and three children
- Spending $500 monthly on clothing
- Reduce the cost of purchased but unworn clothing
- Shop out of season for best pricing
- Savings: $200 monthly

Light Serving

- Single person
- Spending $100 monthly on clothing
- Reduce the cost of buying unneeded clothing
- Savings: $30 monthly

Yield

Servings	Monthly Savings	10-Year × 173	20-Year × 521	30-Year × 1226
Hearty	$200	$34,600	$104,200	$245,200
Light	$30	$5,190	$15,630	$36,780
Your Info				

Nice savings and you still look great! Use the savings to pay off those credit card bills from purchases made before you read this recipe.

Melted Month to Buy

$ $ 🏆

Turns out there's an ideal month to buy just about everything. That includes the obvious, such as saving on snowblowers in April and Christmas decorations in January. It also includes the less obvious—including vacuum cleaners in December and major kitchen appliances in September. Of course, the Black Friday and Cyber Monday deals in November peel prices on just about everything.

A big part of this savings is about going against the flow of other shoppers. People think about buying new cars in the spring and snowmobiles in the late fall. The bargains often lie on the *opposite side* of the calendar. Big savings can be had with just a bit of planning.

This same philosophy can be applied to investing. Guru Warren Buffet suggests, "…be fearful when others are greedy and to be greedy only when others are fearful."[44] His approach of patiently buying low has made him billions. Maybe he started with deals on washers, lawn mowers, and linen, then worked his way up to buying distressed companies.

Ingredients
- Mark your calendar with the best time of year to buy everything. A quick online search will yield this information.
- Book regular planning sessions to optimize major purchases.

---

[44] Warren Buffet, "1986 Berkshire Hathaway Shareholder Letter," Berkshire Hathaway, February 1987, https://bit.ly/3kCMYbi

- Slot those purchases into the optimum months and set calendar reminders to shop in those months.
- Do reviews in advance to narrow down the best make and model for your needs.
- Compare prices both online and in-store to get the best deals.

Hearty Serving
- Family of five
- Spending $2,000 monthly on durable goods
- Buy half of those items in their optimal months: saving 20%, or $200, monthly

Light Serving
- Single person
- Spending $1,000 monthly on durable goods
- Buy half of those items in their optimal months: saving 20%, or $100, monthly

Yield

Servings	Monthly Savings	10-Year × 173	20-Year × 521	30-Year × 1226
Hearty	$200	$34,600	$104,200	$245,200
Light	$100	$17,300	$52,100	$122,600
Your Info				

In the case of a sudden emergency, you'll need to replace something right away, no matter the price. But for most purchases, a pinch of planning and perhaps a smidgeon of waiting could add nearly a quarter of a million to your retirement. That's no small potatoes!

Minced Medical Bills

$ $ 🍴 🍴

Even with medical insurance, health bills can really scramble your budget. I spoke with Angel Cellucci, nurse practitioner and founder of the medical expense firm, Overbrook Consultants LLC for background and ingredients:

- Average annual health insurance deductibles are $4,364 for an individual and $8,439 for a family plan.
- Medical service providers must disclose their pricing, although many do not.
- Eight of every ten medical bills contain errors.
- Medical expenses drive 62% of bankruptcies.

Ingredients

- Stay as healthy as you can to reduce medical procedures. Eat right, get enough sleep, and exercise regularly.
- If you're covered by health insurance, minimize costs by ensuring that all your providers and services are in-network.
- Research and compare medical expenses for both cost and care quality, including: [45]
  - **Procedures**: Knee replacements range from $12K to $53K.
  - **Durable Medical Equipment**: Fracture boots range from $50 on Amazon to $1,500 from a hospital.
  - **Tests**: Brain MRIs with contrast range from $195 to $5,400.

---

[45] Example procedure with local price ranges from Turquoisehealth.com

- Compare cash prices with your cost after insurance.
- After any medical procedure, carefully check the bill for:
  - **Double billing**: Have you been charged for the work more than once? Billed for three IVs when you only had one?
  - **Services not received**: Did each procedure even happen? Were you in the facility at the time and date on the bill?
  - **Upcoding**: Were you billed for full anesthesia when you only had a local?
  - **Unbundling**: Were you billed for individual procedures that could be more economically coded as a single, less costly set?

Hearty Serving
- A family with several chronic conditions
- Carefully check bills for each hospital visit and medical provider
- Shop for cost and quality on each service
- Savings: $300 monthly

Light Serving
- Single person, maintains a healthy lifestyle
- Carefully check bills from hospital visits and medical providers
- Shop for cost and quality on each service
- Savings: $100 monthly

Yield

Servings	Monthly Savings	10-Year × 173	20-Year × 521	30-Year × 1226
Hearty	$200	$34,600	$104,200	$245,200
Light	$100	$17,300	$52,100	$122,600
Your Info				

This recipe pairs nicely with Par-boiled Prescriptions. Yum!

Clarified Comparison Shopping

$ $ $ ¶

Sometimes it's tempting to quickly succumb to a dark purchasing desire. To call the first plumber in the search results. Or lo, to blindly pay any monthly cost without some financial diligence. But buy in haste, repent at leisure. It has never been easier to comparison shop for any kind of product or service.

Ingredients

- Get 3 quotes on any major expenditure. Consider specs as well as cost. Things like home repair can easily swing by 30% or more on price and even more on quality

- Look at online reviews and get personal referrals

- Consult unbiased research sites like Consumer Reports to select products with the best quality, value, and durability

- For smaller monthly purchases, take the time to research alternatives, pricing, and delivery

- Some online services like Amazon's "subscribe and save" can reduce costs by 15% on regular purchases like pet food, laundry detergent and grocery items

- Do some quick online comparison in-store before making a purchase

- For in person shopping, always ask politely if they can do better on price. Never hurts to ask.

- Check online for discount codes before checking out

- See if the purchase qualifies for cash back on rebate sites like Rakuten

Hearty Serving

- Family of five with a home and a cottage
- Get 3 quotes on an average of $15,000 a year on home improvement and repair projects between the two properties
- Save 20% or $3,000 annually, or $250 monthly

Light Serving

- Single person
- Comparison shops on $500 of key household monthly expenditures (vitamins, pet food, haircuts and beauty services, personal care items etc)
- Saves 20% on monthly expenditures
- Savings, $100 monthly

Yield

Servings	Monthly Savings	10-Year × 173	20-Year × 521	30-Year × 1226
Hearty	$250	$43,250	$130,250	$306,500
Light	$100	$17,300	$52,100	$122,600
Your Info				

A quick price check, a Facebook post seeking electrician recommendations or getting 3 quotes on a home improvement project. You got this! Get those savings working for you through debt repayment or increased investment.

Lean Ground Learning

$ $ $ Ⱦ

From cooking to chess to playing the accordion, there are thousands of free and low-cost ways for both kids and grown-ups to learn almost anything through books or online learning options. Live classes are always an option, but now there are numerous low cost virtual alternatives as well.

Don't forget about the library. It's changed a lot—now offering access to physical and online resources, classes, and sometimes even legal and travel assistance.

If you prefer instructor-led classes, Zoom and other free communications apps can connect you with lower-cost options. Or, check out the online options to augment in-person instruction.

Where are you spending money on learning? Let's see if we can skim off budgetary fat while maintain that great flavor.

Ingredients

- For business professional development, check out free podcasts.
- For musical training, try free or low-cost websites.
- For fitness and yoga, consider free or low-cost apps or sites.
- To study a new language, check out free mobile apps.
- For kid's tutoring, look at online academies.
- YouTube offers instruction in everything from building a fence and fixing a fridge to broiling lamb and beating the bongos.

Hearty Serving

- Family with two guitar students and one math student
- Two music lessons at $100 each, or $200 monthly; math tutoring at $60 monthly
- Spending $260 monthly
- Switch lessons to free online classes.
- Savings: $260 monthly

Light Serving

- Single person
- Taking two business classes for a total of $100 monthly
- Sign up for online learning for a total of $20 monthly
- Savings: $80 monthly

Yield

Servings	Monthly Savings	10-Year × 173	20-Year × 521	30-Year × 1226
Hearty	$260	$44,980	$135,460	$318,760
Light	$80	$13,840	$41,680	$98,080
Your Info				

Do an inventory of all your learning expenses and consider digital alternatives to reduce costs and add new possibilities.

Par-Boiled Prescriptions

$ $ $ ☗ ☗

Prescription drugs are a bit of a no-brainer. In to see the doctor, out with a piece of paper with illegible writing. By a small miracle, there's a pharmacy right in the basement or across the street from the doctor's office. Such luck! While the pharmacist fills the bottle, you're checking out Instagram, online news, or the customer in front of you. Still not filled? You check your blood pressure on the little machine or stroll the aisles aimlessly looking at medical devices. Then you get hailed. Your scrip is ready. You ask a few questions about drinking, operating heavy machinery, or taking the pills with peanut M&M's. Then you pay and leave.

What got missed? The price! There's a big cost swing from one drugstore chain to the next and an even bigger one when you check online pharmacies. I realized this when I shopped my statin pills and then wrote a blog post, "How I saved 94% on my prescription drugs."[46] Yes, the difference is *that* big. This becomes critical if you have a chronic condition and need the medication indefinitely. Without a drug plan, this is a big deal. Even with one, this might save you from annual copays or coverage caps. In fact, the difference is so big that paying cash may be less costly than your insurance copay!

Let's press down hard with our palm, twist the cap, and open the bottle on serious cashflow.

---

[46] Gordon Stein, "How I saved 94% on my prescription drugs," CashflowCookbook.com, January 2021, https://bit.ly/3kvjg8e

Ingredients

- Ask your doctor about lifestyle changes that may eliminate the need for a particular medication or treatment.
- Ask for a generic drug prescription if available.
- Call pharmacies and big box stores to check pricing.
- Compare pricing with several online pharmacies.
- Purchase medication in 90 vs 30-day quantities (save up to 30%).

If you don't have a medical plan, 20 minutes of online comparison save up to 80-95% on your prescriptions.

Hearty Serving

- Family of five with no supplementary medical insurance
- Spending $300 monthly on prescriptions (30-day supply)
- Switched to online pharmacy $30 monthly (90-day supply)
- Savings: $270 per month

Light Serving

- Single person with no drug plan
- Prescription costs of $90 monthly at local drugstore
- Found same prescription for $12 monthly, delivered
- Savings: $78 monthly

Yield

Servings	Monthly Savings	10-Year × 173	20-Year × 521	30-Year × 1226
Hearty	$270	$46,710	$52,100	$331,020
Light	$78	$13,494	$40,638	$95,628
Your Info				

Bake the freed-up cash into debt reduction or savings!

Deep-Fried Day Care

$ $ $ ⍵⍵

OK, kids are cute, but raising them comes with many challenges. As they grow and develop, sharing in their triumphs is incredibly rewarding, from their first steps to their Harvard graduation, stellar career and beautiful family. OK, we can dream!

Some of this unbridled joy gets melted by the costs involved. Day care is doubly challenging, since it is a major expenditure and that usually comes during the early career years when money can be tight and there's a lot of rushing to get the formula/vomit/poo cleaned off your clothes as you race out the door at 7:30 AM. Are there ways to trim these costs?

Ingredients
- Check your company benefits program for paid parental leave policies.
- Familiarize yourself with parental leave legislation and benefits.
- Do the math to see whether it's better for the lower-income spouse to stay home with the children or to get paid help.
- Enlist family members to help with day care. Can you barter home improvement labor or other services in return?
- Consider sharing a nanny or babysitter with a neighbor, alternating hosting duties every couple of weeks.
- Comparison shop on day care costs. Consider the quality of care, reputation, and enrichment in addition to costs.

Hearty Serving

- Family with two working adults and two children
- Spending $2,200 monthly on a private nanny
- Move to nanny sharing with neighbors, giving nanny a 20% raise to $2,640
- New day care costs: $1,320 monthly (split with neighbor)
- Savings: $880 monthly

Light Serving

- Family with two working adults and one child
- Spending $1,100 monthly on day care
- Research local day care offerings, find an accredited one with great care for $900 monthly
- Savings: $200 monthly

Yield

Servings	Monthly Savings	10-Year × 173	20-Year × 521	30-Year × 1226
Hearty	$880	$152,240	$305,939	$614,809
Light	$200	$34,600	$69,532	$139,729
Your Info				

* Although a child will normally attend school by age 5, many families with both parents working still require child care outside school hours, so assume a total of ten years of child care. Note that the 20-year value comes from continuing to grow the 10-year value at 7% for another ten years, but without the monthly savings contributions.

Cooked College Costs

$ $ $ ¥

So off they go to college or university—babies no longer. For parents, the void of having no one to nag or drive to soccer practice is filled by an astonishing set of new bills, as well as the October 3ʳᵈ phone call to proclaim that college student of yours needs additional funds. *Now!*

Let's look at more palatable ways of handling the high costs of college.

Ingredients

- Reduce tuition costs by taking AP credits in high school.
- Plan early to weigh the costs of a program and college with the expected income as a graduate. Some options aren't worth it.
- Consider less expensive state colleges or community colleges.
- Start saving early and consider using a 529 plan that includes federal tax savings as well as possible state tax benefits.
- Use scholarship sites to find and apply for scholarships.
- Complete the FAFSA (Free Application for Federal Student Aid)—even if you aren't sure you'll qualify.
- Communicate your parental contribution a few years before college so the student can start saving *their* part. Pay only the hard costs (housing, books, tuition, food) or a percentage of them. Let your student cover her own beer, residence damage, road trips, 3:00 AM pizzas, and concert passes. With this approach, urgent requests for money are eliminated. Your child builds budgeting skills and maximizes summer jobs. Win-win.
- Cover only a fixed number of years of college.

Hearty Serving

- Family expecting a total of ten years of post-secondary costs (e.g., two children in four-year programs and one in a two-year program spaced so there is one child in school each year)
- Total hard costs, $3,000 monthly (tuition, books, lodging, groceries) plus soft costs of $400 monthly for a total of $3,400
- Use scholarship sites to reduce hard costs to $2,500
- Fund only 75% of hard costs or $1,875
- Savings: $1,525 monthly

Light Serving

- Family with one child in a four-year program
- Total hard costs, $2,500 monthly, plus soft costs of $400 monthly for a total of $2,900
- Apply to FASFA and receive grant of $3,000 or $250 monthly, reducing hard costs to $2,650
- Fund only 80% of hard costs or $2,120
- Savings: $780 monthly

Yield

Servings	Monthly Savings	10-Year × 173	20-Year × 521	30-Year × 1226
Hearty	$1,525	$263,825	$530,178	$1,065,436
Light	$780	$65,459	$131,544	$264,349
Your Info				

* The 20- and 30-year values come from growing only the ten-year savings.

** The 10-year savings include 4 years of reinvested savings, then compounding that amount for 6 more years, the 20- and 30-year values come from growing only the ten-year savings

Not reflective of your situation? Look at your base case costs, apply relevant ingredients and update the Your Info row.

Takeout Container - Household

This section offered up ten areas that can save a potential total of $193,998 for our Light Serving and a whopping $698,055 for the Hearty Serving over ten years, when invested at 7%.

✓ **Get creative with the kid stuff.** Find savings in activity fees, team travel, snacks, and equipment.

✓ **Get serious with your cell service.** Optimize wireless plans, use free services, protect devices.

✓ **Stop throwing away money on clothes.** Shop mindfully, buy fewer, higher quality pieces, and limit impulse shopping.

✓ **Be a month miser.** Buy things in the optimal month and save on all kinds of durable goods and services.

✓ **Mash medical expenses.** Consider different options for needed procedures.

✓ **Dare to compare.** Get three quotes on large purchases and look more closely at recurring expenses.

✓ **Learn to learn in new ways.** Consider online and app-based learning, versus in-person, and explore library resources.

✓ **Prescribe yourself lower drug costs.** Ask about generic medications and consider licensed online drugstores.

✓ **Lower the cost of higher education.** Pay the hard, set costs, while your kids pay the variable costs.

✓ **Mind the cost of minding the kids.** Barter with other parents, share nannies, shop around for low-cost care.

Continue to scour household expenses and free up cash for debt reduction and investing for financial freedom. Check out the Ingredients section at CashflowCookbook.com for products and services that can help.

Lifestyle

AFTER YOU'VE PAID FOR INSURANCE, taxes, oil changes and electricity bills, what's next? Maybe you'd like to have fun as well. Part of the bonus of saving on things like groceries and the gas bill is that you can spend some of these savings on things that are actually enjoyable.

Here in the Lifestyle section, we'll look at ways to save on areas that people relish, including:

- Subscriptions
- Gambling
- Family fun
- Fitness
- Television
- Vacations
- Smoking
- Restaurants
- And more!

As always, feel free to skip the recipes that don't apply to you and to use your own assumptions for the savings math. Be sure to get full value from the monthly savings by paying down debt or increasing your savings rate.

Scalded Subscriptions

They begin innocently enough: a magical pathway to a delicious morsel of music, news or video. The little temptresses ask only for the numbers of your credit card for a small amount that can be easily cancelled. Months later, they're still there, hanging out on your card statement, slurping away your cash, bit by bit.

Subscriptions come in all kinds: apps, websites, and services. They offer up music, video, entertainment, instruction, news, and magazines. Often, their promise is forgotten, but the payments are evergreen.

Ingredients

- Check your credit card and bank statements. Make a list of every subscription. Include a description of what they offer.
- Cancel any unloved or forgotten subscriptions.
- Consider moving to a lower-tiered option.
- Try calling and objecting to the price. There's is a good chance they'll lower it.
- Check for duplicate coverage. Did your cell company include Spotify, while you're paying separately for Apple Music? Are you paying for separate Netflix licenses when they allow multiple users?
- Are you paying for multiple subscriptions when one with multiple services might be cheaper? For example, Apple One includes storage, video, fitness, news, magazines, and games.
- Consider paying annually vs monthly for bigger savings.
- Look for a free app with the same functionality as the paid one.

Hearty Serving

- Family with two parents and three children
- Spending $125 monthly on subscriptions
- Eliminate two not being used, saving $25
- Renegotiate one to save another $10
- Combined the rest to a single-family app that covers music, news, fitness, and storage, saving $30
- Savings: $65 monthly

Light Serving

- Single person
- Spending $65 monthly on subscriptions
- Join brother's family plan app, saving $20
- Replaced a paid app with a free version saving $10
- Savings: $30 monthly

Yield

Servings	Monthly Savings	10-Year × 173	20-Year × 521	30-Year × 1226
Hearty	$65	$11,245	$33,865	$79,690
Light	$30	$5,190	$15,630	$36,780
Your Info				

Thirty minutes of assessing, eliminating, combining, negotiating, and replacing, and voila ... wealth through fewer subscriptions. Be sure to lock away the benefits in debt reduction or savings.

Gravied Gambling

It's hard not to get seduced by that $41 million lottery jackpot, the slot machine that's just starting to heat up or that last…wait…second last, poker game. The yacht, private jet, and secluded beach are oh-so-close; there can be no quitting now.

As promising as it sounds, the odds of winning a major jackpot are about ten million to one. A venomous snake bite, being hit by lightning, or kidnapped by radicals are all much more likely—although admittedly less desirable. But shockingly, 60% of US millennials plan on using lottery winnings to fund their retirement.[47]

The average millennial spends $976 annually on gambling.[48] Looks like we're burning a bundle on a blackjack barbecue.

Ingredients

- If you're addicted to gambling and have built up gambling debts, now is the time to get professional help.
- If you're in control, but regularly buy lottery tickets, switch to a sure winner, paying off debt or increasing investment.
- If casino time with your besties is a regular thing, see if you can make that a hike or a spa day instead. Or, switch the venue to each other's homes and play poker for quarters.

For simplicity's sake in the examples below, we will ignore the value of smaller prizes that may be won from time to time.

---

[47] Jeremy Quittner, "Why Saving for Retirement Isn't Playing the Lottery," STASH.com, April 2019, https://bit.ly/3uZ3sk9
[48] Amanda Dixon, "Vices like drinking, smoking and gambling cost Americans more than $2,400 per year," Bankrate.com, December 2019, https://bit.ly/3McHNLc

Hearty Serving

- Two gamblers in the household
- Monthly spend on lottery tickets of $100
- Eliminate gambling entirely
- Savings: $100 monthly

Light Serving

- Single person
- Gambles $45 monthly
- Eliminated gambling entirely
- Savings: $45 monthly

Yield

Servings	Monthly Savings	10-Year × 173	20-Year × 521	30-Year × 1226
Hearty	$100	$17,300	$52,100	$122,600
Light	$45	$7,785	$23,445	$55,170
Your Info				

Looks like passing on lotteries is a solid bet, paying out an estimated $122,600 after 30 years. Might you win the big one with 30 years of ticket buying? Maybe. But the odds are much better when you invest in yourself.

All-Dressed Family Fun

$ $ 🍸

Savings don't show up only in mundane areas like car insurance, gas bills, and groceries. There are easy savings on fun things, too. Here's a delectable easy-to-execute recipe for budget entertainment.

Ingredients

- For high-end live entertainment, consider buying subscriptions vs. individual tickets, or look for group buying deals.
- Try websites that offer reasonably priced local music, small venue theater, and comedy performances, or look for pay-by-donation nights and free preview performances.
- Most movie theater chains have a "cheap night," and cinema loyalty points programs can save cash on admission and snacks.
- For attractions, look at local sites that offer discount tickets.
- Do an online search for the name of the attraction in which you're interested to locate "coupons" before booking online.
- Check with big box membership retailers for discounted event, restaurant, spa, and sports gift cards.
- Check with your employer, alumni association, and automobile association for discounted tickets on events and attractions.

Hearty Serving

- Family of five, spending a total of $233 monthly
- Seeing five high-end theater shows a year, two tickets at $130 each, for the equivalent of $108 monthly

- Visiting family attractions (amusement parks, water parks, etc.) five times a year, for the equivalent of $125 monthly
- Buy two tickets to five less-expensive shows and events through event websites for $25 each, totaling $21 monthly
- Use Groupon passes to save 25% on family attractions, for $94 monthly
- New cost: $115 monthly
- Savings: $118 monthly

Light Serving

- Single person
- Seeing twelve sporting events and theater events each year, averaging $100 per ticket, for the equivalent of $100 monthly
- Dining out at restaurants pre-event for $50
- Total monthly cost: $150
- Switch to employer discounted event tickets at 20% off, for a new cost of $80 monthly
- Switch to Costco discount restaurant gift cards for $40
- New total cost: $120 monthly
- Savings: $30 monthly

Yield

Servings	Monthly Savings	10-Year × 173	20-Year × 521	30-Year × 1226
Hearty	$118	$20,414	$61,478	$144,668
Light	$30	$5,190	$15,630	$36,780
Your Info				

Numerous online resources can help you save on live music, theater, and attractions. Take the time to bookmark useful ones for your location. Enjoy the events and savor the cashflow benefits, too.

Julienned Gym Costs

$ $ 💐

So you didn't end up looking as good as the airbrushed, spray-tanned model on the poster at the fitness club that convinced you to get the three-month-free, act-now-cancel-any-time membership. Dang.

Now your biceps are shrinking, but your expenses are still pumped up by the pre-authorized gym payments. Nothing wrong with gyms if people are using the memberships. But if you're not? Let's get out the blender and liquefy these loot leaches.

Ingredients

- Inventory your fitness memberships. Can any be eliminated?
- Shop around for lower-cost gyms in your area.
- Check out your local community center or YMCA for low-cost or free classes, swimming, or other activities.
- Check your work benefits for a gym subsidy or discount program.
- Search online for bodyweight exercise programs. Who knew you've been carrying your own gym with you all along?
- Hit the online sites and buy lightly used fitness equipment for your home. There's lots of great gear out there being used as laundry drying racks.
- Take up running or biking for nearly-free cardio workouts.
- Look at free workout videos on YouTube or check out free or low-cost apps.

Hearty Serving

- Family with two adults and three teens
- Spending $300 monthly on gym memberships
- Discover an unused employer gym subsidy of $50
- Cancel one membership and use an app, saving $50
- Switch to a cheaper gym for one membership, saving $30
- Total Savings: $130 monthly

Light Serving

- Single person
- Spending $75 monthly on an unused gym membership
- Cancel membership, join running club and switch to YouTube-led, home-based bodyweight exercises
- Savings: $75 monthly

Yield

Servings	Monthly Savings	10-Year × 173	20-Year × 521	30-Year × 1226
Hearty	$130	$22,490	$67,730	$159,380
Light	$75	$12,975	$39,075	$91,950
Your Info				

Flex your saving muscles. A toned and healthy family with dwindling debts and increasing investments. And spare the bottled water and athletic drinks. This pairs best with plenty of fresh, cold, and free tap water.

Tossed Television

$ $ ❦❦

The chronology is a blur. From black and white to color, from rabbit ears to cable, to lugging home the VHS machine and videos (Be kind—rewind! Yeah, right!), to Netflix shipping discs in the mail (How could that work?), to Netflix streaming (That really did work!) to Apple TV, Roku, Slingbox, and Chromecast. And even better, digital rabbit ears.

With all this change, who has time to bake in the lowest costs? You do! Go look at a copy of your TV content bills. Take an hour to figure out for what you're paying and who in the house actually watches what. Odds are someone added a channel package to catch some show that was cancelled three seasons ago. Time to spoon out savings.

Ingredients

- Consider cutting the TV cord entirely. Yes, I know you will miss the ads, infomercials, upcoming show previews, and the reality series about hoarding.

- Switch to the new skinny TV bundles for a light fix of basic cable and local content.

- Look at one of the online providers. Some now include movies, sports, and regular network programming.

- Try Netflix, Amazon, or Hulu for all-you-can-eat TV shows and movies. Once you get used to being able to binge watch episodes, it's hard to go back to one-episode-at-a-time, commercial-laden TV.

- Explore devices like Chromecast or Roku for access to movies, music, content, and more from your TV.
- Look at dedicated apps to follow a particular sport like NFL, NBA, or F1.
- Install a digital antenna if you're in an area with strong over-the-air coverage. Use one of the online tools to check for signal strengths and available channels at your address.

Hearty Serving

- Two properties with two cable subscriptions for $200 monthly
- Move to a digital antenna* for the city home for $0
- Move to Apple TV and Netflix** at vacation property for $14 monthly + four videos monthly at $12, for a total of $62 monthly
- Savings: $138 monthly

Light Serving

- One home cable subscription at $120 monthly
- Moved to a streaming TV package for $65 monthly
- Savings: $55 monthly

Yield

Servings	Monthly Savings	10-Year × 173	20-Year × 521	30-Year × 1226
Hearty	$138	$23,874	$71,898	$169,188
Light	$55	$9,515	$28,655	$67,430
Your Info				

* Yes, there's a cost for a digital antenna—about $300 for a large outside one and $100 or less for an in-home model. Feel free to deduct the cost from the 10, 20 or 30-year savings!

** Netflix may be used in more than one location and multi-user licenses are available—check the latest rules, offerings and pricing.

Tenderized Travel

$ $ $ ¥ ¥

If you're in the habit of enjoying a nice annual vacation that adds to your debt load and sinks you deeper in the hole, you may want to do "staycations" while getting your finances in order. By following some of the other recipes you will be able to build a solid financial base and make vacations fun and affordable.

If you can enjoy a regular vacation while continuing to grow your net worth each year, enjoy. But let's see if we can plate up ways to do it more economically, without taking away any of the fun.

Ingredients

- Use one travel reward card for all work and personal spending to build a plump travel points balance.
- Look at Airbnb, TripAdvisor, and Trivago to find independent lodging and Hotels.com, Priceline, and Hotwire for the best deals on the major hotel chains.
- Choose midweek flights rather than weekends.
- Book well in advance.
- Travel just outside peak season (i.e., shoulder season) for your destination. If you're flexible, look at last-minute travel sites.
- Check for free shuttles from airports to hotels and the city center rather than paying for cabs or Ubers.
- Consider accommodation with a kitchenette, so that you can make meals and snacks, which reduces dining out costs.
- Look at destinations with favorable exchange rates for better local spending power.

Hearty Serving

- Family of five annual vacation (divided by 12 for monthly costs)
- Spending of $858 for air and lodging
- Fly midweek to reduce air tickets from $625 to $525
- Use Airbnb to reduce lodging costs from $233 to $133
- Used travel reward points to save $50
- New cost: $608
- Savings $250 monthly

Light Serving

- One person, annual vacation (divided by 12 for monthly costs) Buy one-week all-inclusive package for $258
- Move trip to shoulder season and pay $208
- Use travel reward points to reduce cost by $25
- New cost: $183 monthly
- Savings $75 monthly

Yield

Servings	Monthly Savings	10-Year × 173	20-Year × 521	30-Year × 1226
Hearty	$250	$43,250	$130,250	$306,500
Light	$75	$12,975	$39,075	$91,950
Your Info				

There are many, many more ways to save on travel and dozens of apps and websites that can help. Check out the Ingredients section at CashflowCookbook.com for new ideas. Stay curious, research each component (air, car, lodging), add new techniques and flavors, and immediately use the savings to reduce debt or add to your nest egg.

Toasted Time-Off Toys

$ $ $ 👥 👥

OK, so you absolutely had to own that cottage/scooter/snow-mobile/sailboat/chalet/ski boat/sports car. But as you look at your finances, you realize the debt could diminish or the savings could soar without the taxes, loan payments, insurance, maintenance, and repair costs being funneled to all of your toys.

On the other hand, dang, it's hard to part with these once you have them! Is there a way to have all the fun with fewer calories?

Ingredients

- If the item is one you can share, why not sell a half interest to a friend or relative? Set up a shared calendar on your smartphones for bookings. Split the work, maintenance, and insurance.

- Can you rent the item to others? Or can you sell it and just rent one when you really need it?

- Can you downsize the item? Sell the big one and get a smaller one online. Set up an alert so you know when the right one comes along.

- Cut the repair costs by getting the repair manual, viewing YouTube videos, or partnering with a technically minded friend to learn how to do maintenance yourself.

- Shop for insurance. Double-check that you aren't paying twice for the coverage.

- For equipment you'll use infrequently (like that tractor you were sure you needed), consider renting it from a building supply or tool rental shop.

Hearty Serving

- Family owns a sailboat valued at $40,000
- Boat is used only on some weekends
- Sell a 50% interest for $20,000*
- Save half the cost of insurance: $67 monthly
- Save half the cost of dock rental: $67 monthly
- Save half the cost of maintenance and sails: $166 monthly
- Savings: $300 monthly

Light Serving

- Family owns an older sports car valued at $20,000
- Use car lightly
- Sell the car for $20,000*
- Save $125 on insurance, $83 on maintenance, and $50 parking and storage
- Cost savings $258 monthly
- Rent a convertible for three weekends for equivalent of $50
- Net savings: $208 monthly

Yield

Servings	Monthly Savings	10-Year × 173	20-Year × 521	30-Year × 1226
Hearty	$300	$51,900	$156,300	$367,800
Light	$208	$35,984	$108,368	$255,008
Your Info				

* Value of debt paydown or savings contribution from selling a toy and value of depreciation savings is not included in yield table.

** Assumes the arrangement would continue for 10 - 30 years

Smoked Cigarettes

$ $ $ 👣👣

If you smoke, you no doubt already receive ample pressure to quit. You're forced outside in the dead of winter, well away from building entrances. You're lectured by your dentist about yellow teeth and gum disease and rejected by your friends for the smell and the endless hacking. The insane cost is just the glowing cherry on top of this misery sundae.

Cigarettes are now about $7 a pack—assuming you aren't rolling your own, sailor-style. For ease of figuring, we'll also leave out increased healthcare costs and just consider the cost of the butts themselves.

Ingredients

- Quit smoking to save your health and maybe even your life, as well as an astonishing amount of money.
- See your doctor for advice on the best way to quit.
- Check your employer benefits and programs for help.
- Consider a shift to vaping to save costs, and to possibly reduce the health concerns. Check first with your medical professional.
- Ask if your employee benefits plan includes smoking cessation clinics.
- If someone else in your house smokes, quit together to increase your chance of success

Hearty Serving

- Household with two smokers
- Each smokes one pack daily, for a total cost of $420 monthly
- Both smokers are able to quit entirely
- Savings: $420 monthly

Light Serving

- Single smoker
- Smokes half a pack daily, for a cost of $100 monthly
- Quits smoking through a work program
- Savings: $100 monthly

Yield

Servings	Monthly Savings	10-Year × 173	20-Year × 521	30-Year × 1226
Hearty	$420	$72,660	$218,820	$514,920
Light	$100	$17,300	$52,100	$122,600
Your Info				

Looks like our "Hearty Serving" couple above could retire with 2 ½ times the wealth of the average American at retirement by just quitting smoking and butting out for 30 years! Yes, you could make a case that smoking helps with retirement planning by reducing the number of years of retirement life to fund, but there are happier routes to financial independence.

Char-Broiled Restaurant Checks

$ $ $ ♈♈

There is nothing like a sunny day on a patio with good friends, great food, and perhaps a massive pitcher of Sangria. And few things can beat a romantic dinner in a beautiful restaurant.

But if you're steeped in debt and your credit card statements look like a bar and restaurant guide, it may be time for adjustments. Let's not take the fun out of everything, but a little fine-tuning on ordering and frequency will chill your bill.

Let's look at a "Fully Loaded" restaurant bill, then make changes for a "Lower Cost" version.

| | | | | | Cost for 2 Diners | |
Menu Item	Item Cost	Tax (8%)	Tip (15%)	Total Cost	Fully Loaded	Lower Cost
Bottled water	$6	$0.48	$0.90	$7.38	$14.76	0
Cocktails	10	0.80	1.50	12.30	24.60	0
Appetizers	12	0.96	1.80	14.76	29.52	14.76
Glass of Wine	12	0.96	1.80	14.76	29.52	29.52
Entrée	25	2.00	3.75	30.75	61.50	61.50
Dessert	12	0.96	1.80	14.76	29.52	14.76
Total	$77	$6.16	$11.55	$94.71	$189.42	$120.54

Ingredients
- Skip the opening cocktail and bottled water (tap water is fine).
- Split an appetizer and a desert.
- Save 37% with these simple changes (see table above)
- Reduce dining out frequency and get into home cooking.

Hearty Serving

- Family of five
- Dining out four times per month, for a total cost of $800
- Switch to two dinners out per month with tap water, no sodas, no appetizers, and no desserts for a total of $325 monthly
- Savings: $475 monthly

Light Serving

- A couple
- Dining out three times per month, for a total cost of $600
- Maintain three dinners out per month, but skip the cocktails, drank tap water, have a single glass of wine each, and split a dessert, for a total of $450 monthly
- Savings: $150 monthly

Yield

Servings	Monthly Savings	10-Year × 173	20-Year × 521	30-Year × 1226
Hearty	$475	$82,175	$247,475	$582,350
Light	$150	$25,950	$78,150	$183,900
Your Info				

Great get-togethers, a chance to explore the city, savor inspiring conversation, and save the dishes, but now at a new low price that allows you to save more than a half a million dollars over 30 years! That's a financial feast!

Larded Lifestyle Inflation

$ $ $ 🍴

Every now and then, our salad of life gets an extra dollop of monetary dressing. Perhaps a barrister from a faraway land sends an inheritance from an unknown aunt. Maybe our mortgage gobbles its last payment. Or, that miserly boss hands us an unimagined raise. Pretty much as soon as the cash arrives (and often before), it is earmarked for new things, accessories for our old things, or trips to give us a new place to buy new things.

Mind you, before the new cash shone upon us, we were doing just fine. Enjoying our life and the scenic view, as we hike up Maslow's pyramid of needs.[49] Before getting used to this new loot, why not set aside a slice to build a lifetime of financial freedom? You won't miss the cash, because, well, you never had it.

Ingredients

- Agree on a fixed percent of any new funds to apply to debt or incremental investment. Twenty percent is a good starting point. Enjoy the rest as a well-earned treat.

- Apply this to income goodies like raises, stock plan payouts, inheritances, and side hustle income. This also works well when a major expense ends, freeing up cash including mortgages, student loans, car payments, alimony, and lines of credit.

- Determine whether your priority is debt paydown or incremental investment, then apply the extra right away. Also,

---

[49] "Maslow's Hierarchy of Needs", Wikipedia, https://bit.ly/3s99qNv

consider using the cash to increase your 401(k), Roth IRA, or company stock plan.

Hearty Serving

- Family with a mortgage payment of $2,000.
- Mortgage gets paid off early, family increases monthly investment contributions by 30% or $600.
- Family enjoys the other $1,400 of cashflow
- Extra Savings: $600 monthly

Light Serving

- Single person earning $100,000
- Gets a 10% raise, or approximately $600/month after deductions
- Apply 1/3 to incremental monthly investment and spend the rest
- Extra Savings: $200 monthly

Yield

Servings	Monthly Savings	10-Year × 173	20-Year × 521	30-Year × 1226
Hearty	$600	$103,800	$312,600	$735,600
Light	$200	$34,600	$104,200	$245,200
Your Info				

The easiest money to save is that which you haven't met yet. Brilliant start to financial freedom.

Takeout Container - Lifestyle

Wow, lots of delicious leftovers in this section! We threw ten ideas on the cutting board to save a total of $167,464 for our Light Serving and $449,108 for the Hearty Serving when invested over ten years:

✓ **Sear the subscriptions.** Look at your household subscriptions. What can get chopped, or combined?

✓ **Stop gambling, start saving.** The surest payoff comes from redirecting your gambling expenses to long-term investments.

✓ **Have fun for less.** Use Groupon, look for discounts and taste great, lesser-known venues.

✓ **Scrape high fitness costs into the compost.** Audit your gym memberships. Consider lower cost alternatives.

✓ **Trim TV costs.** Look at HD antennas and other tricks to enjoy low-cost entertainment.

✓ **Learn about discount travel.** Take advantage of comparative information, the sharing economy, and other travel tricks.

✓ **Share your toys.** Sell, rent out or share expensive trappings to recoup or split costs. Optimize operating costs.

✓ **Butt out.** It's tough to quit, but good to look at the economics, as well as the health benefits.

✓ **Slim down your restaurant spending.** Apply clever ways to slash the bill but not the fun.

✓ **Lose the lifestyle inflation.** Divide your raises among more consumption, rapid debt paydown, and increased investment.

A bit of creativity can open new areas of fun, entertainment, and adventure while reducing costs. Check out the Ingredients section at CashflowCookbook.com for helpful products and services.

Financial

AH, THE FINAL COURSE. There are lots of great dishes to choose from here. In this section, we look at wealth-friendly ideas for all the ways you exchange, transact, invest, borrow, and manage your money. Flip through and see which ones are to your taste.

We'll take a closer look at:

- Bank fees
- Credit card fees
- Life insurance
- Tax returns
- Credit ratings
- Mortgage and debts
- Foreign exchange
- Investment management
- Second incomes

Some of these recipes will be useful right away. Others are worth revisiting as the contents of your financial fridge evolve over time.

Broiled Bank Fees

 $

If your bank has been doing monthly fee-snacking on your account, it may be time to do a bit of cost nibbling of your own.

Look at your last few statements to determine the average monthly cost. Include service fees, withdrawal fees, fees for printing and mailing a statement, item fees, overdraft fees (yes, you!) and any other fees. Do a similar review of your spouse's and kids' accounts. Add up the totals, drop them into the food processor, and julienne them into something more appetizing.

Ingredients

- Shop online to compare fees and services with different institutions. Be sure to consider your banking service patterns.
- Consider paperless banking to streamline your record keeping and possibly reduce bank fees.
- Some institutions waive account fees if you keep a certain amount on balance.[50]
- Meet with your bank representative to review your fees. Get their thoughts on the right account for your needs.
- Consider looking at all your financial business and consolidating this with one provider for reduced costs and better service.
- For students, show your student card when setting up accounts. Most institutions offer no-fee accounts for students.

---

[50] As an example, having a $35 monthly fee waived for maintaining a $5,000 balance is an 8.4% risk-free, after-tax return. Hard to beat!

- Similar savings are available for seniors at the other end of the age spectrum.

Hearty Serving

- Family with two children
- Total monthly account fees, including extra charges, totaling $63
- Move to more efficient account types, for a cost of $24 monthly
- Savings: $39 monthly

Light Serving

- Single adult
- Total monthly account fees, including extra charges, of $24
- Move to online-only account with no fees
- Savings: $24 monthly

Yield

Servings	Monthly Savings	10-Year × 173	20-Year × 521	30-Year × 1226
Hearty	$39	$6,747	$20,319	$47,814
Light	$24	$4,152	$12,504	$29,424
Your Info				

While you're at the bank, preserve this fresh cash by asking the service rep to increase your automated debt payments or savings by the amount equal to your fee reduction.

Chopped Credit Card Fees

 $ ♉

Paying off your credit cards every month is *critical.* At 20%, an ongoing $10,000 balance will cost more than $2,000 each year in interest. Each month brings new purchases, more interest, and an ever-growing balance. It's like a soufflé that keeps rising, oozing from the oven, and taking over the kitchen—almost like a scene from a cooking horror movie.[51]

Take a second job, sell your baseball cards or rent out your basement. Whatever. Just *pay the plastic off every month* and keep the debt soufflé in the oven. With the door latched.

Let's make sure your card fees don't eclipse the value of your card rewards.

Ingredients

- When comparing cards, include the annual fee for the primary card and the second (spousal) card.
- Understand the treatment of foreign currency purchases. What mark-up does the card charge beyond the inter-bank rate?
- Check the value of rewards as a percentage of spending. For example, a card offering $75 for every $5,000 of spending is offering $75 ÷ $5,000, or 1.5%. Not as good as a card offering 1.75%.
- Balance reward value against card fees. Are you ahead?
- Avoid credit card insurance that pays the balance if you die. Get adequate life insurance and don't maintain a card balance.

---

[51] Assuming that there is such a genre. Maybe there should be!

- Research several cards online to find one that best minimizes your costs and maximizes rewards for you.

Hearty Serving
- Two cardholders spending total of $1,667 monthly on cards
- Card fees of $19 monthly
- Card pays 1.2% in rewards, or $20 monthly
- Net benefit, $1 monthly
- Switch to lower-fee card costing equivalent of about $2 monthly and earning 1.75% in rewards
- Uses card for an additional $1,250 in work expenses
- Total rewards: now $51 monthly
- Net savings: $50 monthly

Light Serving
- Single adult spending $225 monthly on card
- Card fee of $13 monthly for premium travel card
- Card pays 1.5% in rewards, or about $3 monthly
- Net cost: $10 monthly
- Switch to no-fee, no-reward card, saving $13 monthly in card fees and losing the $3 reward
- Net Savings: $10 monthly

Yield

Servings	Monthly Savings	10-Year × 173	20-Year × 521	30-Year × 1226
Hearty	$50	$8,650	$26,050	$61,300
Light	$10	$1,730	$5,210	$12,260
Your Info				

Note that the monthly net savings represent the improvement from reducing the cost of the cards and/or increasing the reward benefit.

Layered Life Insurance

$ $ 🍴 🍴

OK, let's see what's cooking in the life insurance pot.

If you have people who depend on your income, you need to protect them if you won't be around. If you're unloved by your beneficiaries and have too much insurance, you may need to protect yourself.[52] It makes sense to look for ways to save on life insurance, but don't skimp on the coverage itself.

Ingredients

- Get enough insurance to cover your funeral cost, pay off debts, and replace your income for the balance of your working years.
- Check coverage from both work and personal policies.
- Using term life policies with a duration that aligns with your needs is usually the most cost effective option.
- Shop policies online to optimize costs.
- Review your insurance needs as your situation evolves.

- Consult a qualified financial professional to assess your life insurance needs.
- Eliminate or reduce a policy only if you are absolutely certain it is not required or if you have other coverage in place.
- Be sure you have adequate disability coverage. In many age groups, you are far more likely to become disabled than to die.

---

[52] True crime fans will get this one!

Hearty Serving

- Couple with three dependent children
- Have personal policies costing $200 monthly, plus coverage through employer
- Retain a financial planner to assess needs
- Discover they have more insurance than required between work and personal policies; reduce and re-shop personal policy online to find that optional extra work insurance is less costly
- Eliminate personal policy, increase work coverage, for a new cost of $100 monthly
- Savings: $100 monthly

Light Serving

- Single person with one dependent
- Check to ensure adequate coverage with existing policy
- Shop the policy online for a better rate with a reputable insurance company
- Savings: $50 monthly

Yield

Servings	Monthly Savings	10-Year × 173	20-Year × 521	30-Year × 1226
Hearty	$100	$17,300	$52,100	$122,600
Light	$50	$8,650	$26,050	$61,300
Your Info				

*You can deduct the one-time fee of a financial planner from the 10-, 20- or 30-year value of the savings.

Thickened Tax Refund

$ $ ¥ ¥

OK, exactly how not fun is this? And yet, year after year, here we are, dealing with taxes. Clearly, not temporary as originally promised.

If you're swapping Eurobond futures while trading renaissance art from your Venetian villa, you need a tax expert. If you own a company and need to know how much to dividend to yourself or how to set up a family trust, you need competent professional help.

But if your returns are straightforward, you needn't pay a fortune—or indeed anything—to complete your return.

Ingredients

- If you have complex financial affairs, a home business, significant investments and/or a family trust, shop around or ask for referrals for a good accountant. Never skimp on skills, experience, or qualifications.

- If your returns are simple—say, a W-2 and a Roth IRA contribution slip—look at the free or low-cost online or app tools to complete your return.

- Tax advance loans are a way of getting some or all your expected refund once your return is prepared. There may be fees and interest payable so make sure that you fully understand all costs.

Hearty Serving

- Family with two adults, plus three children in college
- Use an accountant charging equivalent of $158 monthly to complete all five returns
- Move to less-costly, well-qualified accountant charging equivalent of $58 for the returns
- Savings: $100 monthly

Light Serving

- Single adult
- Straightforward tax return
- Using a tax preparation service with immediate cash back for refund
- $120 fee for completing the return and $180 fee for immediate refund of $3,000 totaling equivalent of $25 monthly
- Switched to using free tax-prep software
- Savings: $25 monthly

Yield

Servings	Monthly Savings	10-Year × 173	20-Year × 521	30-Year × 1226
Hearty	$100	$17,300	$52,100	$122,600
Light	$25	$4,325	$13,025	$30,650
Your Info				

Be sure to consider the tax impacts of all of your financial transactions, or engage an accounting or wealth professional to help. Applying the right tax deductions, filing approaches and tax-advantaged programs can have a significant impact on your wealth.

Crusted Credit Rating

$ $ 🍸

Credit ratings are stealthy. They tend to lie quietly out-of-sight, like the dust bunnies under your fridge. And almost as exciting.

But maybe it's time to take another look at that dowdy credit rating. A good credit rating is the key to getting loans and credit cards, and it also has special powers to lower bills and loan rates. And that's where things get interesting.

Ingredients

- Find out your current credit rating and track it over time.

- Learn about the factors that affect your rating, including your payment history, credit use, duration of credit use, mix of loan types, and applications for new credit.

- Focus on improving your credit rating and check the report for errors.

- Improving your credit rating can reduce loan payments by 20% or more, total loan interest by 75% or more[53] and reduce car insurance costs by up to 50%.[54] They can also impact loan applications, job opportunities, cell phone contracts, home insurance premiums, and apartment rentals.

- A good credit score is like a perfect seasoning that improves every financial dish.

---

[53] Loan savings calculator, myFICO, https://bit.ly/3jYMjkq
[54] Ben Breiner "How Does Your Credit Score Affect Auto Insurance Rates?" Value Penguin, September 2001, https://bit.ly/3xMr7WN

Hearty Serving

- A couple with two cars and a home
- Originally paying car insurance of $155, home insurance of $172, and planning on buying a car in 3 months with loan payments of $900, for a total of $1,227
- Improve credit rating by cancelling unused credit cards, paying bills promptly, and correcting errors on their credit report.
- New payments: $132, $155, and $800, respectively, totaling $1,087
- Total savings: $140

Light Serving

- Single adult
- Improves credit report through on-time payments
- Calls car and home insurance firms to requote
- Saves a total of $65 monthly on the premiums

Yield

Servings	Monthly Savings	10-Year × 173	20-Year × 521	30-Year × 1226
Hearty	$140	$24,220	$72,940	$171,640
Light	$65	$11,245	$33,865	$79,690
Your Info				

These examples are modest. A poor credit rating can cost you hundreds of additional dollars extra each month. Develop a fascination for your credit rating and treat it as you would a loved one.

Deboned Debt

$ $ ¥¥

Whether you collect debts like chefs collect cookbooks or you just carry one or two, there may be an easy way to reduce cost and, hopefully, send those debts down the drain faster.

Build a table that lists all your debts, including the balance and interest rate. Here's an example:

Debt	Balance	Interest Rate
Credit card	$5,600	22%
Car loan	$12,500	12%
Student loan	$56,000	7.2%

At 22%, that credit card debt is about to blacken, stick to the pan, and set off the smoke alarm! If you carried the $5,600 for a year, paying only a minimum monthly payment of $112, you would pay $1,221 in interest. And you would still owe $5,477 on the card. That's gotta leave a bad taste.

Ingredients

- If you have several debts, consider a home equity line of credit (HELOC), and use that to pay off your high-interest debt.
- Of course, always aggressively pay down your highest interest rate loan and be sure to pay off credit card balances each month.

> Don't consolidate all your debts into a lower-rate HELOC and then start assuming new debts or growing your card balances. That defeats the purpose!

Hearty Serving

- Family with credit card debt and student loans
- Monthly payments of $1,110 over ten years at 6% on $100,000
- Move that $100,000 to the HELOC at a 3% interest rate
- New monthly payments: $965
- Savings: $145 monthly

Light Serving

- Single person with $20,000 of credit cards at 23% interest
- Payments of $386, with an estimated ten-year payoff
- Arrange debt consolidation loan at 10%
- New monthly payments: $264
- Savings: $122 monthly

Yield

Servings	Monthly Savings	10-Year × 173	20-Year × 521	30-Year × 1226
Hearty	$145	$25,085	$50,410	$101,304
Light	$122	$21,106	$42,414	$85,235
Your Info				

* Note that the 20- and 30-year savings take the ten-year savings and future value them at 7% for ten and 20 additional years.

Note that the examples are for illustrative purposes. Your loan rates and terms may vary. Do the math for your situation. Is there a way to reduce your interest costs? Don't consolidate only to brew up more debt!

Chicken-Fried Foreign Exchange

$ $ $ ▼

OK, so you're up for a bit of jet setting. Or maybe you freelance in a foreign currency or have a kid backpacking in Europe.

If you regularly find that you need to exchange currencies, it's worthwhile to shop for the best exchange rate. Let's compare an airport FX (foreign exchange) kiosk, a bank, and a discount FX company converting US $1,000 US to Euros and back twice:[55]

Start with $1,000 US	Airport FX Kiosk	Bank FX	Discount FX*
To euros	€740	€854	€874
Back to $USD	$796	$893	$955
Back to euros	€589	€763	€837
Back to $USD	$634	$797	$914

*Note that some of these firms will only exchange bank-to-bank

Wow! Big difference. Are you likely to switch your money back and forth like this? No. But this exercise shows how a lousy exchange rate carves big slices off your cash with each conversion. Focus on the rate and minimize switching. Are you going to renovate your entire financial kitchen to exchange $50? No. But if you regularly change money, you're blessed with foreign stock options, or you regularly receive inheritances from foreign relatives, this is for you.

---

[55] Note that this is illustrative, and rates will very. Rates were gathered on March 30, 2022, and generated from actual airport FX kiosk rates, a major US bank, and a US discount FX firm.

Cashflow Cookbook

Ingredients

- Ask your bank about foreign currency accounts or other options to save on currency conversion fees.
- Use a credit card with favorable FX rates.
- For larger conversions, consider a discount FX company. They usually focus on wiring money bank-to-bank.

> Look up "Norbert's Gambit," a clever way to convert larger amounts of currency between $USD and $CAD.

Hearty Serving

- One person cashing foreign stock options and travelling
- Converting $5,000 monthly at bank rates and converting $2,000 monthly for travel at Airport FX rates
- Switch the $5,000 from bank to discount FX to save $100
- Switching the $2,000 from airport to bank FX to save $300
- Savings: $400 monthly

Light Serving

- One person regularly traveling internationally
- Exchanging $500 monthly at airport FX
- Switch from using an airport FX booth to a bank FX
- Savings: $75 per month

Yield

Servings	Monthly Savings	10-Year × 173	20-Year × 521	30-Year × 1226
Hearty	$400	$69,200	$208,400	$490,400
Light	$75	$12,975	$39,025	$91,950
Your Info				

Barbequed Benefits

$ $ $ 🍴

The book that can dramatically change your wealth isn't a bestseller. In fact, there's a good chance you never read it, even though you got a copy for free if you work in an organization. Behold: Your company benefit book.

Yes, actually hold it. Better still, read it! Between its covers, or within its PDF, lies a whole buffet of financial treats. Many employees leave these benefits on the plate. For Employee Stock Purchase plans (ESPPs), 37% of companies report participation rates of less than 25%.[56] And Americans wash $24 billion down their garbage disposals in unclaimed 401(k) plans.[57] Perhaps most shocking, we scrape $224 Billion in unused vacation time off our plates and into the trash![58]

What benefits are you missing?

Ingredients
- Take advantage of matching 401(k) programs.
- See what pension plan opportunities are available.
- If there is a stock purchase plan, what are the terms?
- Understand the details and options of healthcare plan offerings.
- Check for other benefits, such as college tuition, eyecare, hearing aids, massages, fitness memberships, car rental discounts, etc.

---

[56] "Global Stock Purchase Plan Trends Summary", Deloitte, 2018, https://bit.ly/3EH0tQO
[57] "Missing Out: How much Employer Matching Contributions Do Employees Leave on the Table?" Financial Engines, May 2015, https://bit.ly/3k49SrT
[58] Kerry Jones, "The Most Desirable Employee Benefits, HBR, February 2017, https://bit.ly/3k4Wzrs

Hearty Serving

- Two working spouses with benefit programs
- Free up cash using other recipes to use of financial benefits
- Enroll in one spouse's ESPP (employee stock purchase plan) with a benefit of 15% of $25,000 or $234 after tax.*
- Make full contribution to one spouse's matching 401(k), worth $600 monthly pre-tax, or $450 after tax*
- Savings: $684 monthly*

Light Serving

- Single working adult with a benefit program
- Use stock purchase plan worth 15% of $25,000, or $312 monthly, or $234 after tax.*
- Claim extra health benefits including fitness reimbursement, and eye care worth $70
- Savings: $304 monthly

Yield

Servings	Monthly Savings	10-Year × 173	20-Year × 521	30-Year × 1226
Hearty	$684	$118,332	$356,364	$838,584
Light	$304	$52,592	$158,384	$372,704
Your Info				

*These benefits and tax rates are illustrative only. Tax treatment varies by state and personal situation. Consult a financial professional prior to any investment, including ESPPs and 401(k) programs.

Your employee benefits guide might be the second most profitable book you will ever read! (After this one, of course.)

Infused Investment Returns

$ $ $ 👕 👕 ⏣ ⏣ ⏣

Optimizing the after-cost returns on your investments is critical. Get your apron on and tighten the strings. The most important decision is whether to invest on your own or through a qualified financial advisor. DIY advocates point out that investors can buy funds themselves and save on fees.

But DIY investors who invest in funds tend to have 1.7% lower returns than the funds themselves.[59] Another study suggests that investors with advisors may out-earn their DIY peers by about 3%.[60] How can that be? Because people often mess with their investments, selling when things look scary, then buying them back at a higher price when the outlook improves. A qualified wealth advisor can help reduce these panicked losses.

Ingredients

- Learn about investing and monitor your returns vs benchmarks.
- Have patience. Compound investing is slow but powerful.
- Work with an accredited fiduciary wealth advisor who can:
  - Build a complete financial plan.
  - Diversify your investments according to your profile.
  - Optimize your investments from a tax perspective.

    Regularly rebalance your portfolio.

---

[59] Amy C. Arnott, CFA, "Why Fund Returns Are Lower Than You Might Think," Morningstar, August 31, 2021, https://bit.ly/3xMSC2G

[60] Francis M. Kinniry Jr., CFA et al "Putting a value on your value: Quantifying Vanguard Advisor's Alpha" February 2019, https://bit.ly/3K8GRWy

- Provide behavioral coaching to keep you invested.
- Invest in high-quality securities over the long term.

Hearty Serving

- Investing $1,500 monthly
- Work through a qualified advisor, to earn 7% vs 4% DIY return
  (3% improvement with an advisor, per the Vanguard study).
- An investor earning just 4% in the DIY scenario would need to contribute an extra $630 monthly to accumulate the same wealth as the one earning 7%.[61]

Light Serving

- Investing $1,500 monthly
- Stay invested earning 7%, vs 5.3% trying to time market
  (1.7% improvement based on the Morningstar study)
- An investor earning just 5.3% in the DIY scenario would need to contribute an extra $335 monthly to accumulate the same wealth as the one earning 7%.[62]

Yield

Servings	Monthly Savings	10-Year × 173	20-Year × 521	30-Year × 1226
Hearty	$630	$108,890	$328,230	$772,380
Light	$335	$57,955	$174,535	$410,710
Your Info				

*Note that the 10, 20, and 30-year figures are calculated as the difference of the higher return minus the lower return in the servings.

---

[61] This is an illustrative example of the possible Advisor led vs DIY returns using the data from the cited research studies. Individual results will vary.
[62] Again, just an illustrative example. Your results may vary.

Simmered Second Income

$ $ $ ▼▼▼

Most of our recipes have been about reducing the amount you spend as painlessly as possible. But if you want to spice up your debt repayment or layer on assets more quickly, it's worth looking at ways to add another income to your household. A second income is powerful, since it adds additional cashflow that isn't already spoken for with monthly bills.

This idea tends to raise objections, since it involves, well, more work. Understandable. But might there be a way to earn extra funds at something you enjoy anyway? And why not do something fun, more like a paying hobby? Discover what lights your stove!

Ingredients

- Look at online businesses: blog writing, drop shipping, online courses, music instruction, YouTube channel, Tic Tok or podcasting. Build income through ads or affiliate marketing.
- Tutor students on your own or through a tutoring company.
- Teach a course, either live or through an online site.
- Sell your craft items online.
- Set up a lawn care or snow removal service.
- Rent out a spare room on Airbnb.
- Google "ways to earn extra income" for more examples.
- Claim legitimate business expenses to reduce taxes.

Hearty Serving

- Non-working spouse becomes a dog walker.
- Walks two dogs per day at $32 each, 21 days per month, earning $1,344 monthly.
- Provides an extra $1,000 monthly net.

Light Serving

- Single income earner tutors students part time.
- Earns $27 per hour teaching math for 30 hours each month, earning $810 monthly or $600 after taxes.

Yield

Servings	Monthly Savings	10-Year × 173	20-Year × 521	30-Year × 1226
Hearty	$1,000	$173,000	$521,000	$1,226,000
Light	$600	$90,825	$273,525	$643,650
Your Info				

Not exactly crumbs! This is an especially useful recipe if one spouse is not working. Depending on your circumstances, it may make more sense to work extra hours, apply for a promotion, or get a higher-paying job.

Takeout Container - Financial

Savings on financial services offer mighty tasty ways to grow your net worth and save dough. We looked at ten areas that can save a potential total of $278,530 for our Light Serving and $568,824 for the Hearty Serving—truly a lumberjack breakfast—when invested at 7% over ten years:

✓ **Deal with your bank fees.** Work with your institution to slice your fees. Comparison shop as well.

✓ **Get the right credit card.** Flambé rewards cards that don't generate enough points to cover the cost of the card.

✓ **Ensure you're insured properly.** Determine the right level of coverage and then shop the policy to optimize the costs.

✓ **Stop overpaying for tax services.** Consider doing your own return using tax software if you have a basic return.

✓ **Discover and optimize your credit score.** It can impact insurance rates, loan costs, job prospects, and rental housing.

✓ **Downsize your debt costs.** Set the table with a list of your debts. Reduce borrowing costs with a HELOC.

✓ **Exchange the exchange rate.** Boil down currency costs through fewer transactions and optimized exchange rates.

✓ **Understand your benefits.** Study your and your spouse's benefits to take full advantage of the offerings.

✓ **Optimize investment returns and fees.** Ensure you're getting both a great return after fees and the right advice.

✓ **Do the side hustle.** A second income can be a magical force to pay down debt or add incremental income for investment.

Take the time to learn about the costs related to the management of your finances.

Overall Summary: The Stock Pot

WE'VE HAD A LOT OF POTS ON THE STOVE. Let's summarize the cash value of these dishes. Below are all the categories and their value over just ten years for Hearty and Light Servings. Fill in your results on the right. How did you do?

Category	Hearty Serving Total	Light Serving Total	Your Total
Housing	$280,535	$106,186	
Transportation	348,941	119,197	
Food & Drink	410,702	90,306	
Household	698,055	193,998	
Lifestyle	449,108	167,464	
Financials	568,824	278,530	
Total	$2,756,165	$955,681	

Hopefully, you found room for improvement and you've applied the savings to pare down debt and get your investments rising. Maybe you've even changed the way you look at your finances.

With that complete, we need to ask that critical culinary question:

Did you leave any room for dessert?

CashflowCookbook.com

Once you've completed the recipes in this book, you may have a craving for a little more, like a cappuccino after a nice dinner. Whatever you want next in your personal finance journey, it's a click away at CashflowCookbook.com. Here's what to expect when you get there:

Blog: You've just read a few dozen recipes that can send your monthly recurring expenses to the chopping block.

At CashflowCookbook.com, you will find new recipes in the blog each month. Fewer if it's the weather is great for biking. Some of these provide one-time savings: others are new ideas to reduce ongoing costs. They form a nice complement to the recipes in the book.

Subscribe: No spam. No useless offers. No selling the subscriber list to anyone. Subscribers get new blog posts served to their inbox each month. As new editions and complementary information becomes available, you'll hear about that as well. But it's all at a nice pace—maybe two or three emails a month. And it's easy to unsubscribe.

Utensils: If you need help building debt sheets or wealth trackers in Excel, want to use different future value factors, or otherwise need help to implement the recipes in the book, the Utensils section is there for you. Download a table that shows returns for different types of investments over time. Are your investments ahead or behind the index? Other tools will follow. Check this out and download what you need—at no cost.

Ingredients: At Cashflow Cookbook, we are always looking for fresh ideas to help serve up a tastier financial future. We sometimes discover products or services that can help. Worthwhile ones are added to the **Ingredients** section at

CashflowCookbook.com. We don't accept payment to list offerings, but we may get a referral fee if you check out or buy these products and services.

If you have ideas for content or other recipes, please comment on the blog or send me your thoughts:

gord@CashflowCookbook.com.

Acknowledgements

A BIG THANKS to everyone who has been a part of this book.

Special thanks to my developmental editor, Elizabeth Williams, who spiced up the prose and trimmed the fat throughout, and my copy editor, Linda Popky, who helped make the manuscript rise. My son, Austin Stein, added another helping of editorial support. Scott Kish of KishStudio.com baked the signature hat and the icons.

Thanks to everyone who gave the ideas a stir, including Brent Broadhurst, Angel Celluci, Sandy DiFelice, Mike Dunn, Jim Eplett, Mike Fox, Gurmit Gill, Nelly Ginley, Rolie Hamar, Greg Johnston, Mark Kindrachuk, Kerry Mitchell, Roxanne Pearce, Caleb Rubin, David Sculthorpe, Mark Stevenson, Katie Spiler, Joel Teitelbaum, Scott Vaniden, and Lucy Vasic.

A special thanks to my wife and soulmate, Debra, who brings me love and inspiration every day.

Finally, none of this would be possible without the ongoing support of my friends and family. Thanks for helping me throughout this financial feast.

Public Speaking

I AM PASSIONATE ABOUT helping people improve their finances and I enjoy speaking about this with groups, such as:

- Clients of financial advisors, to help them free up funds for incremental investment contributions to build wealth
- Wealth conferences to add a different perspective on wealth building with minimal effort or sacrifice
- Company employees, to help them learn about financial wellness and reducing their money stress

I'm also available to present keynote speeches at company, industry, and trade events.

For booking availability, fees, and other information, please email speaking@CashflowCookbook.com.

For TV, radio, press, and podcast appearances, please send an overview of the program, audience, and timing to media@CashflowCookbook.com.

About the Author

Gordon Stein, MBA, CFEI, founder of Brookside Wealth LLC, a financial wellness education firm, is an international keynote speaker, blogger, personal finance expert and author. He delivers transformational talks that help people crush their number one stress—their finances.

His mission is to improve financial wellness and help his audience regain focus, balance. and joy in their lives. Gordon combines his trademark wit and storytelling style to speak with employee and association groups, financial advisors and the media about a breakthrough path to financial wellness with no risk, minimal effort, minimal sacrifice, and no budgeting.

In his spare time, he is an avid cyclist, kayaker, downhill ski racer, and not yet great (or even good) guitar player. He lives in Cleveland with his wife, Debra, and their three cats.

Made in the USA
Monee, IL
08 February 2023

26854441R00115